ANATOMY OF A LABOR ARBITRATION

SECOND EDITION

SAM KAGEL

The Bureau of National Affairs, Inc. Washington, D.C.

Library of Congress Cataloging-in-Publication Data

Kagel, Sam.
  Anatomy of a labor arbitration.

  Includes index.
  1. Grievance arbitration—United States.
  2. Grievance procedures—United States. I. Title.
  KF3544.K34   1986   344.73'0189143   86-13632
  ISBN 0-87179-523-x   347.304189143

Printed in the United States of America
International Standard Book Number 0-87179-523-x

Preface

This volume is a "How To Do It" book primarily concerned with the preparation and presentation of grievance arbitrations. It is written for all types of persons who engage in this work: for the nonlawyer and lawyer; for the union steward and business agent; for the supervisor, personnel manager, and industrial relations director. It would also be useful to persons engaged in arbitration in nonlabor fields.

This is not a technical book. The problems exposed and examined occur daily in arbitration practice. Of course, not all the subjects considered necessarily develop in a single case. Many problems are telescoped in the discharge case, which forms the core of this book, in order to indicate how they arise in practice and to permit examination of all of them within the framework of the case.

This book reflects some fifty-one years' experience of the author in the field of industrial relations—as an advocate, teacher, and currently as an arbitrator. As of 1985, the author has acted as arbitrator in over 12,000 cases. The suggestions made herein as to practice and procedure are based on this experience.

Labor arbitration is a field with room for differing opinions as to practice and procedure. Most important is the need to maintain the integrity of the arbitration process. This is the responsibility of the parties, the advocates, and the arbitrator.

This second edition has incorporated the monumental aid of my present office colleagues, Arbitrators John Kagel and Kathy Kelly. Professor Kelly also wrote Appendix A.

For the record it must be written that this book, its contents, and conclusions are solely my own responsibility.

Sam Kagel

San Francisco, California
March 17, 1986

Introduction

Millions of workers in the United States have their wages, hours, and working conditions determined by collective bargaining.

The primary objective of the collective bargaining process is the settlement of differences between employees and employers concerning the terms and conditions of their work relationship. In labor-management relations this process of collective bargaining, after the matter of representation is settled, arises at two points:

1. Deciding upon the terms of the collective bargaining agreement.

2. Settling disputes arising during the term of the agreement. The agreement itself provides only the skeleton, the bare bones of collective bargaining. It is the day-to-day settlement of disputes arising during the life of the agreement that provides the flesh and blood of collective bargaining.

Labor unions and employers have devised various techniques for carrying on collective bargaining; that is, the process of settling their differences. The techniques include:

1. *Negotiation:* meeting together, by themselves, and through discussion arriving at a mutually acceptable settlement of the dispute.

2. *Conciliation and mediation:* bringing a disinterested third person into the discussions between the parties. The third person has no authority to decide the dispute but seeks to aid the parties to reach their own settlement of the dispute.

3. *Economic action:* attempting to direct economic pressure and power to influence the other party's decision on the disputed issue. It can take many forms such as strike, lockout, boycott, picketing, and variations or combinations of these.

4. *Legal action:* obtaining injunctions, filing unfair labor practice charges with the National Labor Relations Board, filing damage suits,

or using other legal devices to affect the respective bargaining positions of the union and employer.

5. *Arbitration:* giving a disinterested third person the authority to render a final and binding decision on the dispute. Arbitration is used to settle grievances arising out of an existing agreement. It is also used to decide the specific terms of an agreement. This is called "interest arbitration."

6. *Political action:* seeking to influence the legislative and executive actions of government as they affect labor legislation and its administration.

In arriving at the terms of the agreement, all of the above techniques may be used, separately or in combination with one another. How well or how poorly the methods are used depends upon the skill and knowledge of the bargaining representatives.

In settling grievances, that is, disputes arising during the term of the agreement, only two of the techniques are ordinarily used, negotiation and arbitration. Rarely, if ever, is conciliation or mediation used at this point; nor is direct political action ordinarily involved in the settlement of grievance disputes. In many instances, the parties have given up their right to use direct economic force by including no-strike and no-lockout clauses in their agreements. If the dispute involves an unfair labor practice or gives rise to a legal cause of action, the parties may use legal action, but its use is limited.

Most collective bargaining agreements provide machinery for the purpose of settling disputes arising during the term of an agreement. These grievance procedures take many forms, but ordinarily the first three or four steps use the "negotiation" technique at progressively higher levels of authority in the company and the union. In these steps the parties themselves, through oral discussion, try to settle the dispute. The final step of these procedures, if settlement fails, provides for "arbitration." At that step the parties say, "We can't settle it. Let's bring in somebody from the outside and have him or her tell us what to do. We will agree in advance to accept his or her decision as final and binding."

This book is concerned with only one of the methods of labor-management dispute settlement: arbitration and primarily as it is used in grievance arbitration. At the outset of our discussion of this technique, certain underlying principles should be stated:

1. The best way to settle a dispute—any dispute—is by *negotiation.* Most disputes are, in fact, settled in this way.

2. Arbitration should be the last resort for the parties, in the same way that courts should be used as the last resort in a legal controversy.

3. Arbitration should never be used as a substitute for negotiation; nor should it be used, except in rare instances, as a device to "save face."

Because arbitration is widely used as the terminal step in grievance procedures, literally thousands of labor and management representatives have had to learn about the process. For many of them, arbitration was a new and confusing way to settle disputes. Undoubtedly, the best way to learn about a new technique is to become involved in it. But opportunities for such a slow (and perhaps costly) growth of skill and knowledge are not always available. The very first arbitration case in which a business agent, union or employer counsel, or management representative is involved may be a case that requires considerable knowledge and skill to satisfactorily handle the dispute.

Perhaps the next best thing to actual experience in arbitration is to sit in on a case and watch its development. This book is an attempt to provide that experience; to let you sit in on a grievance arbitration case, to sit in while the parties to a case are determining whether there is actually an arbitrable issue, to listen in while the personnel officer is discussing a grievance with the company attorney, to hear the union counsel and the company attorney make preparations for the case, and finally to be a spectator at the arbitration hearing itself. But this will be more than a mere demonstration of a case; it will be a vivisection. The example case will be taken apart and its elements examined. Through this process some ground rules will be developed for those who are involved in the arbitration of grievances and valuable insight will be given into the grievance process for those who deal with grievances at any step in the settlement procedure.

The example case concerns Ms. Green. Let it be conceded right now that it is "loaded" in her favor. And that many management representatives would never permit this grievance to go to arbitration. But her "case" has the virtue of simplicity, and therefore lends itself to an uncomplicated and easier study of the anatomy of a labor arbitration.

The use of arbitration is, of course, not limited to the settlement of labor-management disputes. To a large extent, what is said in this book will be helpful to those engaged in any type of arbitration, since the basic principles of determining arbitrability, the determination of the issue, the preparation of a case and its presentation apply to all instances in which arbitration is used to resolve disputes.

Contents

ANATOMY OF A LABOR ARBITRATION

SECOND EDITION

Chapter I

What Is a Grievance
for Purposes of Arbitration?

What is a grievance? There's no easy general answer to this question. The following conversation between a worker and his shop steward will indicate a few of the factors that determine whether a complaint is the kind of grievance that comes within the collective bargaining agreement, or just a complaint for which the agreement provides no relief.

The "worker" has just buttonholed his "shop steward."

WORKER: My foreman is a bum. Every day he gets to be more of a bum.

STEWARD: So what?

WORKER: Well, you're the shop steward, aren't you? I want you to do something about it. He's a bum, and I can prove it.

STEWARD: So you can prove it. I can't do anything about it. Tell him.

WORKER: Look, we've got a collective bargaining agreement with the company, haven't we?

STEWARD: Sure.

WORKER: Well, it gives us a right to make complaints, doesn't it? And we have a grievance procedure, don't we?

STEWARD: Yes, but just because you think your boss is a bum doesn't necessarily mean we have a grievance coming under the terms of the agreement.

WORKER: If you worked with him you'd think it was a grievance.

3

STEWARD: Maybe you'd better tell me what you mean. Does he do anything on the job that violates our contract?

WORKER: I suppose not. He's too smart for that. But he's a real so-and-so. The way he orders you around, the way he looks at you. He's just plain miserable!

The complaint must come within the terms of the agreement

STEWARD: There's nothing in the agreement which says he can't be miserable or be a bum. Now, if his actions as a so-and-so violate the agreement, then you would have a grievance which arises out of our agreement with the company. And we could try and cut him down to size. But unless he does something which provides you with a complaint under the terms of our agreement, there's nothing we can do about your beef.

WORKER: We should change our agreement. Couldn't we include in the agreement that any complaint should be treated as a grievance?

STEWARD: I suppose so. But I'm still not certain it would help in this case. Some agreements do provide that any dissatisfaction of a worker that is related to his work situation or his employment relationship is a grievance. I don't know whether your complaint is related to the work situation. When you say he's a bum, are you talking about him as a person?

WORKER: Of course. He's just that kind of a guy. He'd be a bum anywhere.

STEWARD: That doesn't sound to me like a complaint related to your job. Even if we had broader language in the agreement, I don't think we'd get anywhere trying to call that a grievance.

Comment: As the shop steward points out, in the vast majority of agreements not all worker grievances are grievances within the meaning of the particular agreement involved. To determine whether an employer or employee complaint is a grievance subject to the agreement, it is necessary to first ascertain and understand the facts on which the complaint is based; and second, to analyze the language of the arbitration clause in the collective bargaining agreement with reference to those specific facts.

At the outset it becomes clear, therefore, that it is the language of the agreement that controls the rights and duties of the parties. Throughout this book, it will be evident that the original drafting of the provisions of the agreement relating to arbitration is of prime importance. Such clauses should not be merely copies from other agreements. They should be "custom-tailored" for and by each set of parties to a collective bargaining agreement.

This subject will hereinafter be discussed as it relates to various problems that arise from the arbitration process.

Chapter II
The Arbitration Clause in the Collective Bargaining Agreement

The parties to a collective bargaining agreement should give careful consideration to any arbitration clause that is included in the agreement. It is always better for the parties to think through their own particular situation and custom-tailor a clause to that situation rather than just copy a clause from some other agreement.

Scope of Arbitration Clause

The arbitration clause should provide at least the following with reference to the scope of an arbitration:

The parties should attempt to define as specifically as possible the type of dispute which will be subject to the arbitration clause. The parties may wish to strictly limit the types of dispute or matter which will be submitted to arbitration. Or it is possible that the parties wish to make the arbitration agreement as inclusive as it can be made. In either case it is clear that it is the language inserted in the agreement which will be the controlling language and will decide the dispute subject to arbitration—not the unstated intention of the parties. The following examples show how the scope of the arbitration clause may be broadened or narrowed in accordance with the wishes of the parties:

Assume an arbitration clause that reads: "It is hereby agreed that all matters relating to the interpretation and application of this agreement shall be submitted to arbitration." This narrow and restricted language grants to the arbitrator only the right to apply the agreement as written. If the parties wish to limit the arbitrator's powers to this extent, it is also advisable to add the following clause: "The arbitrator has no power to add to, detract from, or change in any way the provisions of this agreement." To be certain that a narrowly drafted arbitration clause will restrict the arbitrator to an interpretation and application of the collective bargaining agreement, as written, it may be necessary to incorporate in the agreement another clause which states, "This written agreement represents the entire agreement on all subject matters covered herein. Neither party has the right to request arbitration on any subject matters not specifically covered herein."

Assume an arbitration clause that reads: "It is hereby agreed that any questions or disputes arising during the term of this agreement, either out of the agreement or resulting from the relationship of the parties, shall be submitted to arbitration." Such language is a broad grant of power to the arbitrator. Not only matters of interpretation and application of the agreement will be arbitrable but any type of dispute between the parties, whether covered in the agreement or not touched on at all, may be submitted to the arbitrator as being within the scope of the arbitration clause. Under this type of arbitration clause it could be quite possible for the arbitrator to determine new terms of the agreement. For instance, if the agreement calls for a wage reopening clause and the parties cannot agree on the new wage rates, such a dispute would be submitted to arbitration as being within the scope of the language quoted above. And the arbitrator would have the authority to settle, and to make a part of the agreement, the new wage rates.

There is one further type of dispute that the parties should consider. Do they wish to include within the scope of the arbitration clause the question of whether or not a particular dispute is arbitrable under the terms of the arbitration clause? If the parties want the arbitrator to decide questions of arbitrability they should so state in the arbitration clause. The courts of most jurisdictions have ruled that, in the absence of an explicit grant of authority to the arbitrator, only the court has the power or jurisdiction to decide what is or is not arbitrable under a particular agreement. If a phrase granting that power to the arbitrator is included in the arbitration clause, then the courts may be less likely to attempt to take this authority on themselves. (For a discussion of some legal aspects of arbitration see Appendix A.)

If the employer and union wish to restrict the type of questions which should be arbitrated, they should be as specific as possible. An employer should not rely on a so-called management rights clause as a refuge against the possibility that arbitration will only be requested on matters specifically covered in the agreement. Although all questions that might be raised after the signing of an agreement cannot be foreseen, certain ones can be anticipated. For instance, if the parties do not want subcontracting disputes submitted to an arbitrator, they should include an express prohibition to this effect.

It is difficult to overemphasize the importance of the language of the arbitration clause in the collective bargaining agreement or to overemphasize the danger of copying the language for this clause from any other agreement. The facts of each particular collective bargaining relationship are unique. An arbitration clause that may perfectly fit one factual situation could result in grave problems if used verbatim in another situation with different parties, a different industry, and different relationships.

Without the arbitration clause the arbitrator has no authority. All of his authority flows from that clause. The extent and nature of his authority is strictly limited by the specific language of that clause. Because of this, it is absolutely essential that the parties consciously determine exactly what kind of authority and how much authority they wish to grant to the arbitrator.

Other Provisions in Arbitration Clause

The arbitration clause should also include the following:

1. A statement that the arbitrator's award will be final and binding on the parties.

2. A statement that the parties agree to share the cost of arbitration in a certain specified way. The usual arrangement is that the parties share the arbitrator's fee equally. But the clause should be broad enough to cover other costs such as the cost of the reporter, if one is used, the rent for the meeting room, traveling expenses for the arbitrator, and other joint expenses which might result from presentation of the arbitration case. It is usually made clear that each of the parties pays its own expense of counsel, travel for its witnesses, the cost of preparing exhibits, and the cost of its copy of the transcript.

Occasionally the agreement provides that the party who loses the case will be required to pay the entire cost of arbitration. Such a provision is based on the theory that this will prevent bringing frivolous cases or using arbitration as a means of harassing the other party. This type of abuse of the arbitration process is rare. And even if it were common, it is doubtful that this treatment of costs does much to deter abuse. This type of clause presents a further difficulty. In any arbitration case, it is sometimes impossible to say in precise terms who "won" or "lost" the case.

3. A description of the method by which the arbitrator is to be selected: The clause should also provide a method for selecting the

arbitrator if the parties fail to agree upon a selection. Some agreements provide that if the parties do not agree, a named impartial agency (e.g., the American Arbitration Association or the Federal or State Mediation Service) shall provide a panel from which the arbitrator is selected by alternately striking the names so provided. In some states, for example, California, such a list is obtainable from a court.

4. A statement defining whether the arbitration clause provides for a single arbitrator or a board of arbitration. There are conflicting views as to whether the case should be submitted to a single arbitrator or to a so-called board of arbitration, consisting of an equal number of representatives of the employer and the union, with the chairman of the board of arbitration being the neutral selected by both parties.

It is suggested that in most, if not all instances, the so-called board of arbitration adds very little to the efficiency of the arbitration proceeding. The fact remains that the persons sitting with the neutral arbitrator are actually advocates. They represent the parties themselves. They should be called party-arbitrators. Therefore, in most instances, they do not add a neutral or impartial point of view to the proceedings. It is true that in a few cases these party-arbitrators approach the issues as impartial arbitrators and vote accordingly.

It has been argued that party-arbitrators may aid the arbitrator in his consideration of the record, particularly with reference to technical matters that may be involved in the dispute. The countersuggestion is that such aid should be given at the hearings. The arbitrator has the authority to call the parties back into session if he needs some technical aid.

In most instances the so-called "technical aid" is an attempt by argument or even evidence which is not in the record to persuade the arbitrator to rule in favor of one party or the other. What usually happens when there is a board is that the party-arbitrators attempt to bargain with the arbitrator for the decision. And this could result in little, if any, weight being given to the actual record of evidence which was produced at the hearing. If the arbitrator permits himself to be used in such a fashion, the whole point of an arbitration proceeding is lost; namely, that a decision will be made based upon the record. If the parties desire to negotiate or compromise then they are certainly free to do so. But the arbitration process itself should not be used as a vehicle for negotiation with the arbitrator after the case has been submitted for decision.

The arbitration process is a form of private judicial determination which has been adapted by long experience to aid in settling labor-management disputes. It should be preserved for that end, and decisions resulting from arbitration should be grounded upon evidence presented at the hearing; not upon either argument or evidence brought forth for the first time in executive session of the board of arbitration. Nor should the arbitrator be placed in the position where, in effect, he has to bargain with one or the other party-arbitrators to obtain his vote in order to arrive at a majority decision.

5. A clear listing of any procedural rules that the parties may wish to impose on the arbitration process; for example, this would be the appropriate place to set out time limits within which a request for arbitration must be brought, and within which the arbitrator should issue the award following the hearing.

The parties sometimes decide to be bound by procedural rules set out by associations such as the American Arbitration Association. If they wish to do this the procedural rules of that association may be included in the arbitration clause by reference to the rules and a statement that the parties intend to be bound by the rules of that association. If the parties do agree to this, it is important that they understand clearly and completely what is contained in the procedural rules to which they agreed. Occasionally a party agrees to be bound by the procedural rules of a named association without understanding the full impact of those rules.

6. A statement that the parties cannot move to the arbitration step of a grievance procedure unless they have first exhausted all of the other preceding steps. This is often implied by the language and structure of the grievance procedure. But a definite statement requiring the parties to first use the other steps takes care of any possible uncertainty on the subject. Of course, there are some cases in which the parties may wish to bypass the earlier steps. To cover these situations the clause should provide that this requirement may be waived by mutual written consent of the parties. Some agreements specifically provide that if one party does not participate in the grievance procedure the grievance can be automatically moved to arbitration with the arbitrator having the authority to make a unilateral award. Otherwise, if one party refuses to arbitrate the other party will have to go into court and obtain an order compelling arbitration.

7. An unequivocal statement that both the union and the employer may initiate the use of the grievance procedure including the arbitration step. There are some situations in which strict interpretation of the agreement would deny the employer the right to initiate arbitration proceedings. This possibility can be easily avoided by including a positive statement granting the right to both employer and union.

Chapter III
Is the Dispute Arbitrable?

If the parties can't settle a grievance by negotiation, one or the other may consider the possibility of going to arbitration. Having failed to settle the argument, he says, in effect, "Let's turn it over to someone else and let him or her decide it for us." Such a decision should be made only after the moving party has carefully weighed several considerations.

Arbitration is not always the best solution when the parties fail to settle a grievance by negotiation. In some instances it may be better to withdraw the grievance. Many of the considerations that should influence the decision to take a dispute to arbitration will be discussed in Chapter IV, Should the Dispute Go to Arbitration?

But even before that determination, there is one basic question which must be answered by anyone considering arbitrating a dispute: Is the dispute arbitrable under the general arbitration clauses of the controlling collective bargaining agreement, or under the terms of a special arbitration agreement; is this particular dispute one in which the arbitrator has the power to render a valid and binding decision? Put another way: Have the parties given authority to someone else to decide the issues involved in the dispute?

Problems of arbitrability   The following conversation will illustrate how the issue of arbitrability could arise. The same conversation can occur between either union representatives or employer representatives. Both union and employer spokesmen should carefully weigh the points and problems discussed in the illustration.

The conversation involves a situation in which the union referred a dispute on wages arising out of a wage-reopening clause to the grievance procedure in the agreement, and the union requested arbitration; the

11

employer then claimed that the subject matter in dispute was not arbitrable under the terms of the agreement.

COUNSEL: There are many considerations that could influence a decision to go to arbitration. The first question that must be answered is whether the grievance itself is arbitrable.

UNION: What do you mean is the dispute arbitrable? We have an arbitration provision in our agreement. Doesn't that cover all disputes including our wage-reopener provision?

COUNSEL: Not necessarily. After examining your entire agreement, I assume you're referring to this Section 33. It provides for a two-year agreement and further provides that wages may be reopened after the first year for the purpose of amendment. Then your arbitration provision, Section 32, reads: "Disputes arising between the parties during the term of this agreement concerning the interpretation and application of the agreement shall be submitted to an adjustment board and if the adjustment board is unable to agree, then the dispute shall be settled by arbitration."

Is that the section you believe provides for arbitration of the wage reopener?

UNION: Yes. And there's another clause in there that says we can't strike.

COUNSEL: Yes, that's right. There's a no-strike clause.

UNION: Well, since we couldn't settle on wages and we can't strike, why can't we arbitrate the wage-reopener dispute?

COUNSEL: Your employer will probably argue that even though there is an agreement to arbitrate, the interim wage issue isn't the kind of dispute that comes under the arbitration clause.

UNION: How can he do that? The agreement says "disputes," and this is a dispute.

COUNSEL: He would probably argue that this isn't the kind of dispute usually handled through the grievance procedure and that the arbitration agreement only refers to disputes having to do with the interpretation and enforcement of the agreement. Not to make a new agreement term, such as setting a new wage.

Power of arbitrator

As you know, the arbitrator gets his power, authority, or jurisdiction to make a final and binding decision only from the mutual consent or joint agreement of the parties to arbitrate certain matters.

UNION: Suppose management refuses to arbitrate. What can we do?

Decision on arbitrability

COUNSEL: Well, we can see if they will agree to let the arbitrator decide whether the dispute is arbitrable. Or we might have to go into court to try to obtain an order directing the employer to arbitrate. Of course, the court might find that there is no agreement to arbitrate at all.

UNION: Which is better—to go to court or to let an arbitrator decide whether it's arbitrable?

COUNSEL: If we can get the employer to agree, I'd rather leave it up to the arbitrator. We could handle the matter more quickly, and an arbitrator would have a greater understanding than the court of the practical situation involved in collective bargaining relationships.

Comment: Some agreements specifically provide that questions of arbitrability shall be decided by an arbitrator.

UNION: Are there different circumstances when the question of arbitrability comes up?

COUNSEL: Yes. Do you want me to review them for you?

UNION: Yes.

Substantive
arbitrability

COUNSEL: Let's first take up what is called substantive arbitrability. What we just discussed, the wage-reopener problem, is such an example.

UNION: Why is it labeled substantive arbitrability?

COUNSEL: Because the dispute concerns adding a new term to the agreement or changing a term already in the agreement. It concerns the substance of the agreement. And in the case we were talking about, related to a change in the wages already provided in the agreement.

UNION: Which term of an agreement would be related to this problem?

COUNSEL: The scope of the agreement to arbitrate. That is, would it include the right to arbitrate a substantive change in the agreement or not?

UNION: Can you give me some examples?

COUNSEL: Yes. Suppose the clause reads that "any and all disputes between the parties arising during the life of the agreement shall be arbitrated." Then it could be argued that even a new provision or a change in an existing provision could be changed or could be added to the agreement through grievance arbitration.

Suppose, however, that the arbitration clause provides that "only disputes arising out of the interpretation or application of the agreement" are subject to arbitration. Then, as in your case, a dispute seeking to add a completely new provision to the agreement or adding to or subtracting from an existing provision of the agreement would probably not be arbitrable. Unless, as I said, we can get the employer to agree to arbitrate, or at least get him to agree to let an arbitrator decide the question of arbitrability.

Is there an
"agreement"
to arbitrate
anything?

UNION: Does anyone ever argue that there is no agreement of any kind requiring arbitration?

COUNSEL: Yes. While such a situation is claimed to raise an issue of arbitrability, it is not a true issue of "arbitrability."

UNION: Why not?

COUNSEL: Because in this situation one of the parties claims that he is not bound by any agreement requiring him to arbitrate anything.

UNION: Can you explain this further?

COUNSEL: Well, a right to arbitrate arises only if parties have mutually agreed to arbitrate. And if one party says that it was not a party to an agreement to arbitrate, then that question must be settled by a court in accordance with applicable law. The parties, however, can agree to give an arbitrator the authority to settle that question.

UNION: What question would the court or arbitrator decide?

COUNSEL: Whether a party raising this issue is bound by any agreement to submit any dispute to arbitration.

UNION: I have had some cases where the employer agrees that it is bound by an agreement to arbitrate, but it won't do so on a specific grievance because it claims it was untimely filed or not filed by the proper person.

Procedural arbitrability

COUNSEL: Yes. This is referred to as procedural arbitrability. As you know, agreements provide for specified time limits within which grievances must be processed and arbitration asked for. And some agreements provide that the grievance must be filed by the employee, not the union. And when such questions arise, the employer could and may take the position that the particular grievance involved is not arbitrable.

UNION: Who decides such a claim?

COUNSEL: The Supreme Court has ruled that the arbitrator, not the courts, decides such questions.

UNION: How are such questions heard by the arbitrator?

COUNSEL: The arbitrator hears the case on the question of timeliness and whether the grievance was properly filed. Then he or she ordinarily proceeds to hear the case on the merits, usually on the same day.

Based on the entire record, if the arbitrator rules that there is a procedural defect, that ends the case. If the arbitrator finds against the claim of a procedural defect, he or she rules on the merit.

UNION: What is the advantage of proceeding in that manner?

COUNSEL: By hearing the procedural question and the merits at a single hearing, it means that the parties, counsel, and witnesses only have to appear at a single arbitration session.

UNION: What is a "bifurcated" hearing?

COUNSEL: Sometimes the parties want one hearing solely for the procedural question to be decided. Then if the arbitrator decides that there were no procedural defects, a second hearing would be held on the merits.

Issue arbitrability

UNION: In some cases, we are unable to agree with the employer on a statement of the issue. Is this a matter concerning arbitrability?

COUNSEL: No. This is not a true issue of arbitrability. Here the parties have not raised a question of "substantive" arbitrability or that there is no agreement to arbitrate or that the grievance has procedural defects. What the parties differ over is the issue or issues that they want the arbitrator to decide. We will discuss this hereafter.

Agreement provisions as to arbitrability

UNION: All right. Can parties provide in their agreement who is to decide questions of arbitrability?

COUNSEL: Yes. Some agreements provide that any question of arbitrability shall be decided by an arbitrator. And even if there is no such provision, procedural questions are always decided by an arbitrator.

UNION: Let me get something clear. Who decides the issue of arbitrability other than procedural arbitrability when the parties do not provide in their agreement that the arbitrator can do this? And when the parties do not voluntarily submit such questions to the arbitrator?

COUNSEL: In federal law the courts have held that, where the parties do not agree otherwise, the issue of arbitrability, except for procedural questions, is for the courts to determine. I have written some comments on this problem. Here is a copy. (At this point, read Appendix A. The *Steelworkers Trilogy* cases referred to in Appendix A are reproduced in Appendix B.)

UNION: At what point in the grievance procedure should a question of procedural arbitrability be raised?

COUNSEL: Some arbitrators have held that the parties must raise the issue of procedural arbitrability at one of the grievance procedure steps prior to the arbitration hearing.

UNION: Do you think this is good practice?

COUNSEL: No. If this is required, it may hamper efforts to settle the grievance through negotiation. Rather than run the risk of losing the right to raise the issue of arbitrability after negotiations have failed (if they do fail), the parties would feel compelled to argue this technicality early in the negotiation steps of the grievance procedure, thus possibly interfering with genuine attempts to settle the dispute without resorting to arbitration.

UNION: Do some arbitrators have a different view?

COUNSEL: Yes. Other arbitrators permit the issue of arbitrability to be raised for the first time at the arbitration hearing. Because this issue is crucial only if the parties do, in fact, resort to arbitration, the right to raise it for the first time at the hearing places neither party at a disadvantage and yet has the positive value of freeing the negotiation steps of the grievance procedure from unnecessary technicalities.

Comment: Because questions concerning arbitrability are the source of so much confusion, a method of analysis is suggested here. The parties should consider their situation in terms of four questions. These questions, and their effect on arbitrability are shown in the chart below. Note that in

	A	B	C	D
1st Question	Do the parties have an agreement that calls for Arbitration? Answer to Question 1 is YES.			
2nd Question		THEN: Does the problem involved come within the scope of the arbitration agreement?* Answer to Question 2 is YES.		
3rd Question			THEN: Have all the procedural steps required by the arbitration agreement been taken in proper time or waived?** Answer to Question 3 is YES.	
4th Question				THEN: Has the *statement* of the issue been agreed upon? YES or NO.
Conclusion	A YES answer to Question 1 only is not enough to conclude that a particular dispute is arbitrable.	A YES answer to Questions 1 and 2 makes it possible to tentatively conclude that a dispute is arbitrable.	A YES answer to Questions 1, 2, and 3 establishes that the dispute is arbitrable. But note possible effect of Question 4.	If answer is YES to Questions 1, 2, and 3, dispute is arbitrable. If answer is NO to Question 4, the right to arbitrate remains, but the problem of statement of the issue remains to be settled by the parties or by reference to the arbitrator, as discussed hereafter.

*This raises the question of "substantive" arbitrability.
**This raises the question of "procedural" arbitrability.

Column A the parties have asked only the first question; in Column B the first two questions, etc.

———

Checklist:
Arbitrability

When confronted with a possible problem as to arbitrability, the parties should ask themselves the following questions:

1. Is there in existence *any* agreement to arbitrate? If this question is in dispute, then ordinarily it is a matter for the courts to decide. (Though the parties could agree to submit such a question to an arbitrator for decision.)

2. Is there a dispute as to whether a particular dispute comes under an arbitration agreement, even though both parties agree that they are bound to arbitrate?

If this is the nature of the dispute, then the parties should further explore:

- the language of the arbitration agreement.
- the nature of the particular dispute.
- whether there is any express or implied agreement to submit issues of arbitrability to an arbitrator, if no general agreement to do so exists.
- the federal law, the law of the state or territory as to who (the arbitrator or the court) has authority to determine an issue of arbitrability in the absence of an express agreement that the arbitrator shall have the authority.

Chapter IV

Should the Dispute Go
to Arbitration?

When a grievance has been processed through all the negotiation steps of the procedure without being settled, the parties must consider whether or not they should take the dispute to arbitration. And while most collective bargaining agreements provide arbitration as the terminal step in the grievance procedure, it should not be resorted to automatically. In fact, many cases go to arbitration that should have been dropped before that stage—even though they hadn't been finally settled.

Assuming the dispute is clearly arbitrable, what do the parties need to know to decide whether they should go to arbitration? They should consider at least all of the following:

- What kind of a case does the complaining party have, is it strong or weak?

- Does the case include a general principle which must be decided because of the possibility of other similar fact situations arising in the future work relationship?

- Is the dispute important enough to justify the cost of arbitration?

- Is there a satisfactory arbitrator available for the kind of dispute involved?

- What will be the consequences of various possible decisions? (Don't always assume the arbitrator will give you the decision you believe should be forthcoming.)

- Is this the kind of case in which the complaining party could "win the argument but lose the battle"? (That is, What will be the effect on future labor relations and on negotiations of future agreements? A favorable decision on one dispute or the nature of the necessary evidence that will have to be produced to win may raise additional problems that outweigh the value of the single victory.)

- Is the issue something which could be taken up more effectively during agreement negotiations?

The following two conversations, (1) between an employer attorney and personnel manager, and (2) between a union representative and union counsel, will illustrate factors that the parties to a dispute should ordinarily consider in order to decide whether or not they should go to arbitration.

The case they are considering involves the grievance of Ms. Green which the union and management were unable to successfully settle in the negotiation steps of the grievance procedure.

> MANAGER: We've got trouble at one of our stores.
>
> COUNSEL: So?
>
> MANAGER: Yes, we've got a lady clerk, Ms. Green, down at the Z grocery store who we claim quit. Now the union has put in a complaint and claims that we discharged her.
>
> COUNSEL: Do you have a *joint fact-finding* procedure with the union?
>
> MANAGER: No. (Read Chapter V, Joint Fact-Finding.)
>
> On top of that, she's claiming that her May paycheck should have included sick leave payments for the time she was sick last month. She also claims she was discriminated against because of her sex.
>
> We've tried to settle this thing with the union, but we aren't getting anywhere. The union wants to go to arbitration. What do we do now?
>
> COUNSEL: I'll need to look at the agreement covering your store before we do anything else. Do you have a copy with you?
>
> MANAGER: No. I didn't bring down the agreement. I don't have an extra copy of it but I had my secretary knock out a copy of a couple of the sections and here they are.

**Agreement
must read
as a whole**

COUNSEL: I appreciate that, but I'm going to have to see the entire agreement.

MANAGER: Why? This gives us the clauses involved; the sick leave provision, the clause dealing with the discharge procedure—and the no-discrimination provision.

COUNSEL: I have to see the entire agreement, not just what you think is pertinent in the agreement. Often the agreement has other provisions which may apply or be related to the dispute. I can't even consider the case unless I have the entire agreement and can analyze it from all four corners to see what I think is relevant or applies to the issues.

I haven't all the facts yet, but first of all I want the entire agreement, not just those three sections.

MANAGER: All right. I'll be glad to send it to you.

COUNSEL: Be sure and do that. That is the key document. I want to study it.

Comment: The practice that an agreement should be read from "all four corners," that is, each and every provision of the agreement, cannot be overemphasized. Arbitrators have sometimes found that after a case had been submitted and the arbitrator has had occasion to study the agreement, certain provisions of the agreement which had been overlooked by both parties, either affect the case as presented, or in some instances would have settled the dispute without the need to go to arbitration.

COUNSEL: In addition to that I will also want some of the agreements for maybe the three or four years preceding the present agreement.

MANAGER: What for?

**History of
development
of provisions**

COUNSEL: Well, you have a dispute here concerning certain agreement provisions and I'd like to know just how the agreement provisions developed and—

MANAGER: I don't think these sections have changed at all.

Examine all documents

COUNSEL: Well, I appreciate your "thinking" on that, but I want to be sure they didn't change so I'd like the agreements for at least four years back.

And also I want copies of any exchange of letters between you and the union on these disputes. Were there any letters on it?

MANAGER: Yes.

COUNSEL: Do you have any copies with you?

MANAGER: No.

COUNSEL: Well, I'll need them, so bring them along when you bring the agreements. Now, you said you met with the union on this. Are there any minutes or reports on those meetings?

MANAGER: I think so, but I'll have to check with the office to be sure.

Grievance file

COUNSEL: Bring along whatever you have in writing on it. And, if she filed a formal grievance, I'll want to look at that, too. In order to advise you on this matter, I must examine all these documents. Any one of them might include crucial material.

MANAGER: Okay. You'll get them.

———

Comment: It is of the utmost importance that a complete file be kept of every grievance. Such file should include copies of the current agreement; any expired agreements which may be relevant to the dispute; copies of the written complaint and any written answers to the complaint; all correspondence dealing with the dispute.

Official minutes of adjustment or grievance board meetings should be examined. Such minutes should be approved by appropriate signatures of the parties, before being considered as the official minutes. In the absence of official minutes, the parties should make and retain complete and accurate notes of the proceedings at such meetings.

———

Get the facts

COUNSEL: Now that we've got that out of the way, let's consider the sick leave pay claim first. What are the facts on that?

MANAGER: Last month she was out Friday the 1st, Saturday the 2nd, Sunday the 3rd, and Monday the 4th. Only two of those days were scheduled workdays, Friday and Monday. She came back to work on Tuesday.

The agreement says we pay sick leave if the sick leave extends beyond a three-day period. We claim that means three working days and the union is claiming it means three calendar days. And there were only two scheduled workdays in the four days Ms. Green was out.

Understand the issue

COUNSEL: And the problem is that she was out for four calendar days.

MANAGER: That's it exactly. The language is clearly in our favor.

COUNSEL: Well, if it's so clear, why the argument between you and the union? You tell me the agreement provides for sick leave after a three-day period. Does it read three calendar days or three working days?

MANAGER: Neither, it just says three days.

COUNSEL: That's the point. The language is not clear. It's ambiguous. It could mean either one.

MANAGER: Well, how do we clear it up for the arbitrator?

COUNSEL: If we can convince the arbitrator that the language is ambiguous, then he or she should allow us to put in evidence of "past practice," and, if it would help clarify its meaning, evidence on the negotiation history of that clause.

Ambiguous language and "past practice"

Comment: Language is considered ambiguous if it can be read as having more than one meaning, either by itself or in the context of the agreement or on other evidence. If a party can establish his claim that the language is unclear or ambiguous, then he should introduce past practice and the history of negotiations if they support his interpretation of the language. The purpose of this evidence is to aid the arbitrator in resolving the ambiguity. And the manner in which the parties have applied the language in the past is a good key to what they intended the language to mean.

Weight should be given to the past practice in interpreting the language of the provision if it has occurred with sufficient frequency and notoriety that it is, or should have been, known to both parties.

For example, an agreement provides that a discharge grievance must be filed within five days of the discharge. Grievant A files a grievance seven days after his discharge. The employer claims that the grievance is untimely. Past practice in many cases shows that the parties have never counted weekends as part of the five-day notice. Accordingly, since the agreement did not identify the nature of the "five days," whether calendar days or workdays, the grievance would be considered timely.

If the practice remained reasonably constant before and after negotiations in which one of the parties had proposed, but failed to obtain, a change in the language of the provision, it will be accorded significant weight. The very existence of an opportunity to negotiate a change in the clause in contract negotiations after the clause was accepted, even though neither party chose to do so, would lend some weight to the contention that past practice was consistent with the meaning that the parties gave to the language in the agreement.

Many times both parties will claim that the language is not ambiguous. Each will argue that it is very clear, that is, if his view of the agreement is adopted. In such instances the parties should provide evidence about the past practice of applying the provision, if any, and the history of negotiations of this provision. Such evidence may help the arbitrator determine the intent of the parties. If the parties do not, and if the arbitrator concludes the language is unclear, he or she may request that evidence.

COUNSEL: Let's leave the sick leave issue then until I have a chance to look at the agreement and other documents. And get me the past practice and history of negotiations on the sick leave provision. Maybe we can agree to submit this issue by briefs. That would save some expense. What about the discharge problem?

MANAGER: We didn't fire the lady. She quit.

Interview the witnesses

COUNSEL: How do you know that? Were you present when the incident occurred that led up to this grievance?

MANAGER: No. You know I have to cover 15 stores in this area. I wasn't there when it happened, but Red—he's the manager—was there and he told me everything that happened. He told me that this lady just picked up her coat and quit. And then she came back the next day ready to go to work. Red told her then that he couldn't use her because he had hired somebody else. And then Red told her she was going to be discharged anyway for not following store rules.

COUNSEL: I certainly want to interview Red and get all the information I can from him.

MANAGER: You mean I've got to take him off the job? You know I've only got a couple of clerks and a manager on at that store. If I take Red off, it doesn't matter what day, it's pretty rough. And he'll start screaming if I ask him to come down on his day off.

Comment: There is no substitute for getting the facts "first-hand." To get the information from any other "secondhand" source may lead to distortion. The distortion may result from forgetfulness or misinterpretation, but in many situations the witness may hold back some of the facts, or color them somewhat if he is telling the story to his immediate supervisor. After all, if the witness was involved in the dispute, he's on the spot, too. And even in interviews with the witness himself, facts may be colored or forgotten for the moment if the supervisor of the witness is present. If witnesses are interviewed privately and separately the advocate has a far greater chance of getting a frank, complete, and honest statement. This is essential for the advocate to better judge the merits of the case and to properly plan its presentation.

COUNSEL: Well, that's up to you. I'd prefer to have him in my office. Then, if I want to, I can have my secretary take down his statement.

MANAGER: He told me what happened. I can tell you. Don't you want to hear the story?

Witness: importance of selecting

COUNSEL: I know, but it won't do any good. I'd like to get the general story from you just for the purpose of analyzing your agreement when I get it, but it's Red who will be the witness at the hearing. Not you.

MANAGER: You mean you're going to have to use him as a witness?

Problem of hearsay

COUNSEL: I certainly will. He's going to tell what happened. Only Red can testify to the facts. All you can testify to is what he told you were the facts and that would be "hearsay." The union won't let us get by with that. They will want the man who was on the scene at the time so they can cross-examine him.

MANAGER: Okay. I'll have to arrange for that, too, then.

Hearsay "evidence"

Comment: Hearsay evidence testimony is given by a person who "heard someone else say something." It is not something that he, the witness himself heard or viewed. It is "secondhand" (thus hearsay). It is generally given less weight than the testimony of the original speaker or actor. This does not mean that the witness giving the hearsay evidence is not to be believed. But he or she is one or more times removed from the original utterance of the words in question or from the action involved in the incident in question.

A witness is put on the stand to tell his or her story. The other party and the arbitrator can test recollection and credibility by "sizing up" the witness (this is called observing the witness' demeanor) and by cross-examination. Clearly these methods are inapplicable when used with the one who "heard someone else say" something. It is the "someone else" who would be the best witness.

As a general rule, hearsay evidence is not allowed in a court trial. Courts usually require that the original witness be brought in to testify. But if this is impossible, the court must determine whether, as a matter of necessity and as an exception to the general rule, the hearsay evidence can be admitted. Thus the right to introduce hearsay evidence must be argued in each case. Although it continues to be a bothersome technicality, the courts have substantially limited the effect of the hearsay rule by establishing numerous classes of exceptions to the rule, and if counsel can argue that the offered evidence falls into one of these exceptions, the hearsay will be admitted in court. In arbitration hearings, the "rule" is more realistic and practical. Hearsay is usually permitted if it is relevant, but is given less weight than would be given if the original observer were testifying. Hearsay is not as persuasive as original evidence; by its nature there is no opportunity to cross-examine or rebut the substance of the hearsay. If the "hearsay" is offered in the form of a written statement, it would be excluded on the basis that there is no opportunity to cross-examine the author of the statement.

In view of this problem an advocate should, whenever possible, avoid the use of hearsay. He should prepare his case intensively, always seeking the original evidence, the primary witness, in short, the best, the strongest evidence to support his case.

COUNSEL: Were there any other witnesses to this incident?

MANAGER: No, I don't think so. Red would know, but I think it was just between the clerk and the manager.

COUNSEL: As far as you know, where did the incident take place?

MANAGER: Apparently all over the store. The way I understand it, from what Red told me, he had asked her to wash the front doors. We have those push-in glass doors and the little kids get their hands on them and they get sticky and dirty two or three times a day, so he asked her to wash the glass and she wouldn't do it. She said that under the agreement she didn't have to do that kind of work, that's for the janitor to do. And that led to an argument and—

Counsel: Let me stop you there for just a moment. Was there anyone present when that happened? Did Red say anyone was present?

Manager: He didn't say. I understand the argument was in the back of the store.

Counsel: Well, your understanding isn't enough. This is one other point to illustrate why I want to interview Red, to find out whether there were other witnesses to this argument.

Manager: All right. Then they got into this argument in the back of the store and then Red—you know what kind of a guy he is—he's a darn good manager but once in a while he gets excited. But anyway, then he—

Counsel: I gather from what you just said he's an excellent store manager but sometimes lacking in good relationships with his personnel.

Manager: You'll see what I mean. You see—

Counsel: That's another reason I want to see Red, to find out what kind of a witness he will be, whether he's hotheaded or even-tempered or what.

Manager: Well, he's redheaded.

Counsel: You mean he's inclined to blow up sometimes? We may find that Red's wrong.

Manager: He'd better not be. We can't afford to have him wrong. We're having too much trouble with this union and we might have to back this guy, right or wrong.

Counsel: Wait a minute. If this is going to be a "face-saving" arbitration, let's consider it carefully.

This is not a matter to be taken lightly. If Red is wrong, is it better to go to arbitration and lose, or is it better to straighten Red out and make him understand the requirements for a normal, intelligent employer-employee relationship?

After I analyze this case and make a recommendation as to whether we do or do not have a good case to bring to arbitration, I want you to really consider this matter carefully. I want you to weigh the possibility of losing the arbitration. Sometimes the consequences of winning or losing are very serious matters.

Face-saving arbitrations

Comment: It is recognized that at times so-called "face-saving" arbitrations may be in order. They should not be used, however, solely because one or the other of the parties is afraid to tell those that he or she represents that they are wrong. The attitude that any union member or supervisor "right or wrong" will always be supported is injurious to the union or to the employer. And the arbitration process should not be resorted to because a union or employer representative may lack the courage to take a position.

MANAGER: I see what you mean. We'll talk about that again after you've talked to Red. I can see now why you have to have all this material and why you have to talk to Red himself.

COUNSEL: Experience has taught me that an employee, in talking to a person in charge, like you— you do have the authority to hire and fire employees such as Red, don't you?

MANAGER: Oh, yes, absolutely.

COUNSEL: This type of employee may often tell you a story to cover up his own mistakes. If Red has made a mistake, I want to find out about it because if I can't find it out from him in our conference, the union will find it out when we are in the arbitration hearing. We don't want to be taken by surprise. You can see that.

MANAGER: Yes, you're right. That could be pretty damaging.

COUNSEL: Now, I interrupted your story with respect to the argument in the back of the store.

MANAGER: Well, Red told Ms. Green, "Look, we've got a report on you that you were not giving out register slips with the packages." After that, according to Red, she really blew her top and grabbed her coat and ran out of the store, or walked out of the store, I'm not sure which, and she yelled that she was being discriminated against because she was a woman.

We figured she just plain quit, but the union is insisting that she was discharged.

COUNSEL: So the union is going to contend in this case that she was discharged and discriminated against and you are going to contend she quit. And I assume that you deny discrimination.

MANAGER: Yes, Well, what else did you want from me? I've got to get back on the job.

COUNSEL: You spoke of a report on register slips. What kind of report was that?

MANAGER: Well, you know we have the Detective Company that sends around shoppers for us who gives us reports on the clerks. One of the reports said that this Ms. Green wasn't putting the register tapes from the cash register machines into the bags. She works at one of the check stands.

COUNSEL: I see. Who hired the detective agency?

MANAGER: I did.

COUNSEL: Do they work solely for you?

MANAGER: I guess they work for other stores, too.

COUNSEL: Do they go to all your stores?

MANAGER: Yes, they go to all our stores.

COUNSEL: As I understand it then, this mistake was observed by a shopper from the Detective Company.

MANAGER: Yes, that's right.

Get facts from primary source

COUNSEL: Then I will want to interview that person, too.

MANAGER: I don't think I can manage that. The agency won't tell who the shopper is. I don't even know myself.

COUNSEL: Then how are we going to prove the incident that occurred with respect to the slips?

MANAGER: They gave me the report.

COUNSEL: We'll need that report but that isn't enough.

MANAGER: What's the matter with the report? This is a licensed detective outfit.

Use of documents as evidence

COUNSEL: The union can't cross-examine a written report. They will want to cross-examine the person who saw what actually occurred. I want to have that observer present. At the arbitration, the union may ask that the shopper be present. The union could object to this report going in without a foundation being laid by the person who made it. I need both the shopper who made the report and the report made to the detective agency.

MANAGER: I can give you the report.

COUNSEL: Is that the same as the report the shopper made or did the supervisor of the detective agency make out a report to send to you after reading the shopper's report?

MANAGER: I don't know that.

COUNSEL: Well, we'll have to find out. I will probably need the shopper and whoever made the report that came into your possession, if it was not made directly by the shopper.

MANAGER: You make this sound like a felony case. Why do you have to have all these things?

Careful and detailed investigation

COUNSEL: No matter how simple the matter may be, most of our work is in the proper preparation of the case. And actually in any grievance, if the facts were investigated this carefully in the early stages of the grievance procedure, you might not have to take as many cases to arbitration. How can you properly handle and evaluate a dispute unless you've made every effort to find out exactly what happened? We're going to have to analyze thoroughly all the evidence to see whether we should go to arbitration.

MANAGER: All right. So far you want copies of the present agreement and you want a copy of the past agreements and any minutes of the grievance meetings.

COUNSEL: Correct.

MANAGER: You want to talk to the manager of the store.

COUNSEL: That's correct.

MANAGER: You want a copy of the report I got from the detective agency and then you want to talk to the person who prepared the report for the detective agency and maybe the shopper who was actually the one who saw her neglecting to put the slips into the packages. Right?

COUNSEL: That's all for the present. And I want that as quickly as possible. The union will probably press for this arbitration to be heard as soon as possible since it claims it is a discharge case. And don't forget, they will probably claim back pay. We don't want to let this thing drag on any more than the union does. It could be expensive for us.

MANAGER: That's right. Is there anything else you want?

COUNSEL: Not for the present. Examining the various documents and interviewing the witnesses may lead to something else I want. If I do want something, whom shall I call upon? You or the store manager?

MANAGER: You better call on me.

COUNSEL: All right. I don't want to have to work with two or three people. If possible, I'd like to work with one person.

MANAGER: You better phone me. How fast can we get going on this?

COUNSEL: As soon as we can get all the information. Get me the written material as soon as possible and we can start on that.

MANAGER: I'll get those to you right away.

COUNSEL: And then I want to talk to Red; the sooner the better.

MANAGER: I'll take care of that. I'll get going on it right away and if there's anything else, you'll call me.

COUNSEL: All right. Fine. As soon as I have all the necessary information I'll be in a better position to advise you about whether or not we should go to arbitration.

Comment: It will be noted that counsel is seeking to obtain all the information possible on the dispute. Only with this information can he:

1. Determine whether there is a "good case."

2. Begin the preparation of the case for arbitration.

3. Understand the case well enough to develop a preliminary theory of the case; know whether he will argue the case on a technical theory or whether the case is stronger on an equitable basis, that is, on a basis of fairness and justice.

Note, again, that counsel repeatedly insisted upon examining all the written documents, in their entirety, before making any judgments concerning the correctness of his client's position on this particular grievance. He was not satisfied to hear about the documents or to see sections of them. He required, for his complete and thorough examination, all written materials which might have any bearing on the case. Counsel also insisted upon personally interviewing everyone who had any information about the case, including the employer participant in the grievance, the shopper from the Detective Company, and the author of the report of the detective agency that was submitted to the store.

Only if counsel is given the opportunity to make and then does make this thorough preliminary investigation of the case will he be in a position to intelligently advise whether the dispute should go to arbitration, or whether it would be better to settle on the other party's terms or at least seek to reach a negotiated settlement. It is often at this crucial point that arbitrations are won or lost. And even more important, if all disputes were thoroughly investigated and considered at this stage, many cases that should never have gone to arbitration would not have done so. In fact, if at the negotiation stages of the grievance procedure, the parties had themselves made such a thorough investigation as is suggested here, the case might have been settled by negotiations without the need to refer it to arbitration. In addition to getting the facts and deciding how strong a case the party has, there are other factors to consider before deciding whether or not to go to arbitration.

————

Assume that the local union official involved in the clerk case has gone to a higher union official or a union attorney for advice and that they have already reviewed the facts and are going on to other considerations:

Time limits
in agreement

COUNSEL: Well, it looks like we have a fairly good case, but before we make any definite move on this let's talk about a few other points. I notice your agreement provides for certain time limits within which this grievance had to be processed. Were those time limits observed?

UNION: I guess so, nobody has raised any questions about that.

————

Comment: Grievance provisions contain time limits within which the grievances much be filed and processed. Any deviation from time limits or agreements to change the time limits should be agreed to in writing by the parties. This will prevent either party later raising the claim that the "statute of limitations" set forth in the agreement has been violated.

————

COUNSEL: If there are time limits in the agreement, we'd better observe them carefully. If one party goes over the time limits and the other party does nothing about it, the time limits might not help at all. I remember one case in which this was a crucial issue.

In that case, the employer went past the time limits, and the union that had filed the grievance didn't claim a default. The parties then agreed to arbitrate. And when the hearing was held, the first thing the union did was to ask the arbitrator to rule in its favor because the time limits were not observed. The company claimed that the time limits had been waived or forfeited.

UNION: What did the arbitrator do?

COUNSEL: Here, I'll read part of his opinion on this point:

> "Time limits that may be set up in an agreement for the processing of grievances are meant to be observed by the parties as they are specified in the agreement. And when either or both parties continue to operate under the grievance procedure beyond the time limits set forth, it is clear that whatever right they may have had with reference to such time limits they have determined to waive. In this case, both the union and the company, by their conduct with reference to certain of the grievances, waived any rights they may have had with reference to the application of time limitations."

UNION: I see what you mean. I'll remember that. There's something else I've been wondering about. If we do decide to go to arbitration, how do we get an arbitrator?

Choosing an arbitrator

COUNSEL: Well, there are a number of persons around here who have acted as arbitrators. They have had experience; they have learned the ropes, so to speak, and by their past awards have shown that they are fair men or women who try to decide cases on the record. The union and employer representatives can usually pick an arbitrator from this group.

UNION: Yes. But suppose you don't have such a group, or you can't agree on someone in the group? Is there any place you can go to get suggestions?

COUNSEL: Yes. There are several sources that can be consulted with respect to obtaining the names of prospective arbitrators. One is the Federal Mediation and Conciliation Service. They give you a panel of arbitrators, if you request it, from which the parties can choose one. Also some State Conciliation Services supply lists. Another source is the American Arbitration Association which provides a similar service.

UNION: Suppose you do have a list of names—how do you decide on the particular person?

COUNSEL: Usually either by mutual agreement or by picking one by lot.

Comment: The method of choosing an arbitrator from a submitted list of names varies. The parties may jointly examine such a list and agree upon a selection. They may alternately strike names from the list with the last remaining name receiving the appointment as arbitrator. Or they may put the names in a hat and draw one of them who is then appointed as arbitrator.

COUNSEL: One problem with lists is that we may not know everybody on it. We'll have to look carefully at the biography sheets that came with the lists. Also, I'll want to check with others who may have used these arbitrators for their recommendations as to how they may have handled cases like this. I'm not so much concerned what the ruling was, but I want to learn how the arbitrator handled the hearing and how sound his or her reasoning was in support of the decision.

UNION: When you are picking an arbitrator, how would you decide which is the "best" one?

COUNSEL: It depends a lot on the type of case you may be arbitrating.

UNION: Take this dispute, for example. If we can get it to arbitration, one issue has to do with interpretation of language in an agreement. So, would you pick a lawyer?

COUNSEL: Not necessarily. Some lawyers may not have any or enough background in everyday labor relations. But if they do, then an attorney might be preferable. However, there are nonlawyer arbitrators who can do the job.

The main thing is to get someone who can interpret and apply agreement language in a fair and sensible way.

UNION: The employers suggested a guy who used to represent employers. I'd never take a man like that.

COUNSEL: I don't agree with you. I always like to have a person who has had practical experience in labor relations. I don't care if he got his experience representing employers or unions.

Union: How could they be impartial?

Ignorance and impartiality

Counsel: Don't equate "ignorance" with "impartiality." I'll never forget the case I had in which the employer ruled out individuals by groups. He wouldn't have professors, politicians, judges, lawyers, social workers, government employees, former employer or union representatives.

Union: Did you get an arbitrator?

Counsel: Yes, a retired Rear Admiral of the Navy.

Union: What happened?

Counsel: He gave the union a fine award. The employer made a terrible error. He thought that in order to be fair and impartial the arbitrator had to know absolutely nothing about labor relations, or to have had absolutely no experience in that field. He equated impartiality with ignorance.

Union: Do you have to get a different arbitrator for each kind of case?

Counsel: No. Some persons have had enough experience as arbitrators in the field of labor relations so that they can qualify for almost any kind of case.

Union: What about the dispute we have now. Do you think we can get a good arbitrator for that?

Counsel: Oh, yes, I think so.

"Splitting" decisions and cost of arbitration

Union: Would the fact that the arbitrator would have two issues lead him to give us one and the company one so he would not make either of us mad at him so he would get picked by us again?

Counsel: We often hear that. But its not of concern. Not if we choose the right arbitrator. A "pro" won't count cases, he or she will "call 'em as he or she sees 'em." That's all we can ask for—to decide each case on the record.

But that does bring up the whole matter of cost of arbitration. One part of the cost of arbitration is the compensation for the arbitrator. Obviously we want an arbitrator who is able, competent, and experienced. Remember, the arbitrator is usually a professional person, a specialist, and must be paid accordingly. You shouldn't go bargain hunting for this kind of service.

Fees of arbitrator

Comment: Arbitrators' fees vary. There should be no hesitancy to discuss fees with prospective arbitrators. Ordinarily arbitrators charge a flat fee for hearing time, that is, so much per hearing day. And an hourly rate for study time. If traveling is involved he will charge for travel expense and travel time.

Parties generally know or can ascertain the range of prevailing rates for arbitrators' fees in their community, and may be able to learn the charges made by a particular arbitrator before contacting him.

Union: Some of our members think that arbitrations cost too much.

Counsel: I know. That's why I'm explaining this to you. If you decide an issue is important enough to arbitrate, then you'd better be prepared to spend some money on it.

Union: I guess there's the legal fee if we have counsel present our case?

Counsel: You're right, that should also be considered as a part of the cost of arbitration. There's also another cost item. And that is the transcript of the hearing. If we want the arbiter to decide the case on the record, we have to give him a record.

Union: Yes, but that's pretty expensive, isn't it?

Counsel: It isn't really as expensive as it seems. After all, if we're going to a lot of trouble and expense to prepare and argue the case, we want to be sure that the arbitrator has all the facts and arguments we presented in a form that he can review at the same time he makes his decision. And that means you should have a reporter to provide a verbatim report of the proceedings, the testimony of the witnesses, so that the arbitrator will have a clear and complete record at the time he decides the case.

And, if there is a lawsuit for some reason over this case, and there are more of these all the time, a verbatim record will show the kind of job we've done to process our grievance and could save a lot more trouble and possible expense.

———

Comment: There is always much discussion concerning the cost of arbitration. The parties can control this situation. If they would do a good or even better job at the various negotiating stages of the grievance procedure, they could avoid arbitration and, therefore, its costs. The use of joint fact-finding would substantially reduce the cost of processing a grievance. But obviously some matters must go to arbitration. And as to these items the cost of arbitration is purely a relative matter. The long-run cost of leaving a dispute unsettled may be considerably more than the cost of arbitration. Or, the presentation of a case, when costs rather than quality are considered more important, will probably not yield the result the parties seek.

When the parties must resort to arbitration, there are ways of keeping costs down, but not by short cuts or gimmicks that prevent the arbitration process from properly functioning. Nor should costs be cut by sacrificing a full and fair hearing, so that the case is decided on the basis of something less than a complete record. The best way to cut the costs of arbitration (short of avoiding it completely) is to fully and carefully prepare the case. This will shorten the hearing time and the time required by the arbitrator to study the record.

The steps in the preparation procedure which are discussed elsewhere in this book that are likely to reduce the cost of arbitration include the following:

1. Thoroughly investigate the grievance. This might lead to settlement.
2. Stipulate to as many facts as possible, thus reducing hearing time. (See Chapter V, Joint Fact-Finding.)
3. Consider alternative ways of presenting evidence (e.g., exhibits, depositions, even limiting the number of witnesses.)
4. Prepare witnesses in advance of the hearings so that their examination is direct and short.

5. Know your case so thoroughly that you can present it in a rapid, efficient, and orderly manner.

6. Perhaps the case can be presented by briefs so there would be no need for a formal hearing or transcript.

It must be emphasized again that while costs are important, they should be considered secondary to maintaining the integrity of the arbitration process. This means providing a full and fair hearing, and a complete record from which the arbitrator should be required to make his decision. If the dispute is worth taking to litigation, that is, arbitration, it is worth going "first cabin." Otherwise settle, compromise, or withdraw the complaint. (See Appendix E, Re Transcripts.)

Location

UNION: Where will the hearing be?

COUNSEL: That's more or less up to us and the employer, although we should ask the arbitrator if he has any preference. We should get a hearing room which will be large enough and comfortable enough so everybody will be reasonably comfortable and so that the arbitrator will have the right facilities. It isn't too hard to find. Hotels have meeting rooms or some arbitrators have offices large enough to hold their hearings there.

UNION: Okay. Well, listen, I'm going to report all this to the Executive Board and see what they think.

COUNSEL: All right. Let me know as soon as you can what you decide about going to arbitration so we can meet our time limits. If we are going to arbitration, there's a lot more work that has to be done. Oh, two other things before you go. The arbitrator we pick very probably will have a crowded schedule so, especially with a discharge case, we want to select one as soon as possible. Another reason to get on the case now is because nowadays arbitrators, because of those crowded schedules, charge cancellation fees. So, if we can settle, we should do so well in advance of the hearing date.

Scheduling and cancellation fees

Comment: Some arbitrators charge cancellation fees if hearings do not go forward on their scheduled dates unless advance notice of a specified number of days is given. Some do not charge if the reason for postponement is beyond the control of the parties, such as illness, or if they can fit in another case on short notice. But the reason for the charge is to allow the arbitrator to fully utilize his or her time. If the parties settle with sufficient notice, many arbitrators can substitute another case for the cancelled one. Parties often will not get down to settling their case until just before the arbitration hearing is to take place. This should be avoided so that acceptable notice of cancellation of the hearing can be given the arbitrator within the time limits he or she sets for cancelling the hearing.

Unfair representation and discrimination

UNION: By the way, you know Ann Green hasn't been the best union officer I've seen. She seems to cause more problems than she solves. She's pushy. We may get somebody with a swelled head if she gets back on the job. Maybe we ought to drop the case.

COUNSEL: Hold it! I know you've had a tough day, but those thoughts are way out of date. You've been around too long to really mean them. Unions have a positive obligation under the law to handle each grievance on its own merits. So the union can't be untimely or even misplace a file or it might be sued for unfair representation.

The Union's duty is now to look at each case in deciding whether or not to pursue it to arbitration. You can drop it, but only if from an objective evaluation of the facts it looks like nothing will be gained from arbitration. You don't have to take any case to arbitration, but you've got to make that determination in good faith. Political reasons or discrimination is *not* good faith. We've got a legal obligation to thoroughly investigate the case and *then* make the determination whether to go or not go to arbitration on its merits only.

Comment: The impact of unfair representation and discrimination concepts as part of the determination as to whether or not to go to arbitration—as well as its impact on arbitration itself—is now well known. But it seems to be little understood.

Both of these matters may not let the arbitration process be what it traditionally has been said to be—final and binding with only limited possibilities of appeal. Unlike arbitration where the union represents the individual employee against the employer, in the lawsuits the individual employee may be suing *both* the employer and the union.

"Unfair" representation cases

In the unfair representation case the union is being attacked for unfairly representing the employee—in bad faith, arbitrarily, or discriminatorily—in the grievance or arbitration process. To prevail against such a claim the union must overcome the employee's claim by showing the even-handed, professional manner in which it has proceeded, such as in its decision to take the case to arbitration, the thoroughness of its preparation, and the professionalism of its presentation.

"Discrimination" cases

A discrimination claim may result from actions similar to unfair representation or may include charges such as bias against women in terms of job promotion opportunities, by seeking to uphold negotiated work rules which do not fairly take into account an employee's religious beliefs, or matters such as preferences in the wearing of hair, clothing, or jewelry. In these situations, the individual has a right to a court trial on the claim, even if he or she has lost at arbitration, although in certain circumstances the court may give weight to the arbitration decision in making its determination.

From all of this has arisen the erroneous notion that all cases must be taken to arbitration. That this is not so is illustrated by the UNION-COUNSEL conversation above. But it has also led to a practice which is an abuse of arbitration: that the arbitration case itself is a form of "insurance policy" against suit, or if one is brought, success in it. Accordingly, cases known to be without merit are nevertheless pursued through arbitration with loss of productive time and money. All cases in an industrial climate do not have merit, and reasonable and fair screening must occur. And if it does, arbitration of the screened out cases need not take place. A union should, as part of its integral service to its members, establish such a screening process and be willing to defend it, if necessary.

If a case goes to arbitration, the union should, if it has merit, vigorously pursue the discrimination claim. But a mere bold statement that discrimination has taken place, without evidence to back it, will be, of course, of no weight.

If a discrimination claim is present, then the safeguards for a full and fair hearing should be redoubled—thorough investigation and preparation and meticulous presentation. A transcript is even more vital to preserve for the court what occurred during the case, in addition to the numerous, other reasons for it, discussed further in this book. The arbitrator should be asked to address the discrimination issue in the decision, and an arbitrator with experience in handling such matters should be selected for the case. Since legal problems are presented, legal counsel should either be consulted or be selected to put the case on.

NLRA claims

A parallel situation involves a case which has either been "deferred" by the National Labor Relations Board or involves a situation which might go before it. The same mode of preparation and presentation is required. The arbitrator should be alerted to the situation and should be requested to address it in his or her opinion. The same legal considerations also apply.

Public sector

Along the same lines, the methodology in this book is equally applicable to arbitration cases in the public sector as well as in the private sector. Particular attention must be paid to the legal aspects of cases in certain jurisdictions, however, especially cases involving federal government agencies. In such instances it is vital that the parties provide full copies of all laws and regulations on which they rely to the arbitrator, after they themselves have achieved a thorough understanding of them. (See Appendix A.)

Checklist:
Should the Dispute Go to Arbitration?

The following is a summary of some of the prearbitration considerations which should be discussed and weighed before final determination to proceed to arbitration. This process should be pursued by both the employer and the union, with their counsels if they use them, or within their own circles if they do not use an outside counsel.

The checklist includes the following:

1. Examine the agreement, the correspondence, the complaint. In short, thoroughly examine all the written material that might bear on the arbitration proceeding.

2. Obtain as many facts, and not secondhand facts, as possible at this stage of the consideration, at least enough to evaluate your case and develop a preliminary theory of your case.

3. Check time limitations, if any, affecting the various steps in the grievance procedure.

4. Consider the type of arbitrator that might be selected in the specific case in question, and how he or she might be selected.

5. Consider the relationship between the type of case involved and the arbitrator who might be selected.

6. Decide what kind of a case is involved, solely one of agreement interpretation, or one that could also include equity considerations, as in disciplinary cases.

7. Determine the probable cost of the arbitration: the arbitrator's fees, the attorney's or representative's fees, cost of transcript, rental of the hearing room.

8. Consider the effect of winning or of losing the case.

It is the weighing of all these factors (and the weight will differ in every case), which should determine whether the grievance should proceed beyond the negotiation stage to the terminal point of arbitration itself. There can be many instances where the weight of any one or a combination of the above factors would lead to a decision to avoid arbitration, even though the moving party believes that it has a "good" case, which could not be settled in the negotiation stages of the grievance procedure.

Chapter V
Joint Fact-Finding

Commentators and parties complain about the cost of arbitration. The aim should be to contain costs while maintaining the quality of arbitration. The length and cost of arbitration is within the control of the parties. The responsibility of the parties, counsel, and arbitrators, in this regard, is noted hereinafter.

One important item concerns the operative facts of a dispute. Too often, these are not known to the parties until the arbitration hearing takes place. Many of the facts could have been stipulated to if the parties had jointly investigated the dispute immediately after the grievance was filed and *before* the arbitration hearing.

Joint fact-finding described below has the following benefits:

1. The relevant facts are jointly ascertained within a short period of time from the date of the dispute.

2. The parties at the negotiating steps of the grievance procedure can address themselves to the relevant facts, not to what "my man or woman" said or did not say. The negotiators are then in the posture of jurors rather than litigious advocates. Settlements of grievances are more easily obtained, thus avoiding the need to go to arbitration.

3. The results of joint fact-finding lessen the political aspects of a grievance. It takes the union representative off the hook if the joint fact-finding establishes that the grievance is without merit. And if the grievance is valid, management can use it to straighten out a supervisor who may have acted incorrectly.

4. The joint fact-finders are instructed to seek only the operative facts which led to the grievance, that is, what actually occurred that caused the grievance. They are not to seek to change or interpret the collective bargaining agreement as written.

Experience in those industries that use joint fact-finding establish that many disputes which otherwise would be arbitrated are settled by the parties without the need to go to arbitration. And if arbitration does become necessary, the first exhibits in the hearing are the jointly found facts eliminating or reducing the need for the use of witnesses. If there are no disputed facts, all that remains for the hearing is argument by both parties. If there is a disputed fact, then evidence is taken only as to such disputed fact.

In the San Francisco Bay Area, where the soft drink industry is represented by six Teamster local unions, joint fact-finding has been used for over 12 years. The number of cases going to arbitration have been very substantially reduced. And in cases where arbitration hearings are held as a result of the joint fact-findings, the arbitrator can hear up to five cases in an ordinary hearing day.

The implementation of joint fact-finding in the soft drink industry occurs when the employee fails to settle the grievance directly with his supervisor and then files a written grievance. This act triggers the fact-finding step. The following outlines the fact-finding process as contained in an agreement in the San Francisco Bay Area soft drink industry between the employers and six locals of the Teamsters Union:

"The fact-finders shall be organized and function as follows:

"(a) One fact-finder shall be designated by the employer and one fact-finder shall be designated by the union.

"(b) The object of the fact-finders is to thoroughly investigate the grievance so that their report could be the basic source of stipulated facts concerning the grievance. Thus the fact-finders shall mutually interview witnesses, including the grievant and the employer representative involved in the grievance, collect relevant written records, and carry out such other investigation as may be required by the specific grievance.

"In the event an employee is appointed by the union as a fact-finder, the employer shall perform his fact-finding function with a minimum interruption of work. Except in discharge and suspension cases, the fact-finding shall be performed on non-working time unless it is impracticable to do so.

"(c) The fact-finders shall put in writing all the facts upon which they agree and these will be considered stipulations. If the fact-finders cannot agree on certain facts, each fact-finder's view of such disputed facts shall also be placed in the written report.

"(d) Upon the conclusion of the fact-finders' investigation and written stipulations, they shall thereafter, within 1 working day, seek to settle the grievance and shall have the authority to do so.

"(e) If the fact-finders are unable to settle the grievance, they shall give to the manager of the plant and a designated person in the union a copy of their written report. The manager (or his representative) and the union representative shall then, within 2 working days thereafter, meet for the purpose of seeking to resolve the grievance."

Chapter VI

How to Prepare the Arbitration Case

When should you start preparing for arbitration? Clearly, part of the preparation takes place during the preliminary investigation which is required before the parties can decide whether or not to take the case to arbitration. But the real preparation begins even before that. It begins the moment the grievance occurs. The way the first line supervisor and the shop steward or business agent handle the problem is part of the preparation of the case. If all grievances were thoroughly investigated and carefully handled at the very earliest stages, far fewer cases would go to arbitration (see Chapter V, Joint Fact-Finding). In effect, everything that is done or said at any stage of the grievance process becomes a part of the case preparation.

After the preliminary investigation, and after weighing all the pros and cons of taking the case to arbitration, if the parties do decide to go to arbitration, there are additional preparatory steps before presenting the case at the arbitration hearing.

The following conversation between an employer attorney and his assistant will illustrate the various steps involved in the final preparation of the case. The same conversation might take place between union representatives preparing the case. The counsel and his assistant are discussing the grievance of Ms. Green, which was the subject of the conversations in the previous chapter:

> COUNSEL: You haven't worked on an arbitration case before, have you? We have one in the office now, and this is as good a time as any to get started. I want you to work with me on this case which concerns a clerk at one of our client's stores.
>
> ASSISTANT: All right.
>
> COUNSEL: It looks now as if this case will involve three issues. Was the clerk discharged, or did she quit;

is she entitled to sick leave pay for certain days when she was out ill; was she discriminated against because she was a woman?

Here is a brief statement of facts that I had prepared after interviewing the personnel manager.

I'll tell you what I want you to do. First—

ASSISTANT: Wait just a minute—since this is my first case I wonder if you would go through all the steps you would take to prepare the case. I think I'd learn more that way than just to have you tell me what you want done. If I don't understand what you mean or why you do something, I'll ask questions.

COUNSEL: All right. That's a good idea.

Analyze agreement; apply agreement to facts

Here's what I do. First I take the agreement and analyze it from all four corners. Generally your client will indicate what he considers the pertinent provisions of the agreement, but quite often there are other related provisions in the agreement that might have been overlooked. So I insist upon analyzing the entire current agreement. In doing that, I work out the relationships between the relevant sections and then see how they apply to the facts that have been given me. When that's been done, and I'm certain I've identified the provisions of the current agreement, then I take the preceding agreements and compare those provisions to see what changes occurred over the years.

ASSISTANT: How do you do that?

Analyze agreement changes

COUNSEL: Well, for instance, let's take Section 15 of this agreement. Section 15 concerns the right to discharge employees, and that will certainly be a crucial section in this case. I want you to trace that section back through all the preceding agreements between the parties. Note any changes of wording that occurred in the section. You might have to hunt for it in each agreement because the section numbers don't always stay the same.

ASSISTANT: I see. I would make a record of all changes that have been made in that section. In short, you want a history of the provision.

COUNSEL: Yes, but more than that. If no changes occurred, I want to know that, too.

If you find changes occurred in the agreement then we're going to have to find out why they occurred. To do this, you'll have to dig for appropriate witnesses and refresh their memories as to just why those changes took place, what happened in negotiations to affect those changes at that particular time, and why the changes were made. And find out, too, if the union or our client made any proposals for changes that each failed to get. That could be valuable information.

That will give us a picture of the development of the agreement terms. Remember, the agreement is the key document. We have to understand how that agreement affects our management rights and which, if any, of our rights it clearly protects.

ASSISTANT: I can certainly see that. I hope the personnel manager has a file of past agreements.

COUNSEL: Probably he does. But if not, you'll have to find out who does. Also see if there have been any past grievances or arbitrations between the parties on the same kind of issues we have in this case. These could be very important to us.

Historical file of agreements

Comment: Every employer and union should maintain a continuous history of their collective bargaining agreements. Changes in the agreement and additions or deletions should be documented. Pertinent dates and reasons for alterations should be noted in writing. An accurately annotated set of agreements will pay important dividends. They will save time in conducting negotiations, and in the handling of grievances and arbitrations. They will make available a clear picture of the development of the provisions.

Parties will, at times, seek to obtain conditions through grievance arbitration which they failed to obtain in negotiations. This should not be permitted. This can usually be prevented if the negotiation history concerning the provision in issue is offered as evidence at the arbitration hearing. Likewise, a good record should be kept of all past grievances and arbitrations.

COUNSEL: Now about the witnesses—

ASSISTANT: Just a minute, I note you have some other documents on your desk. Could we go through all the written material first?

Analyze record of grievance

COUNSEL: I was going to come to those later, but since you raise the point, let's go through them. During the course of these grievance matters there are usually meetings between the parties. I always try to learn whether minutes were kept at these meetings. In this particular case the minutes were not jointly approved. These minutes of the meeting were prepared by our client so we look at them with a questioning eye. The union might claim that they are inaccurate. But they do give us a summary of what occurred and how the grievance developed through the grievance procedure.

I want you to analyze those papers carefully from the point of view of the argument that the employer is making. Then check back in the agreements to see if those arguments are supported by the agreements.

And then I want you to analyze those grievance minutes from the point of view of what the union is contending. We will have to anticipate as best we can the union's arguments, the union's point of view, and what it relies upon. That's the only way we can prepare our own affirmative case and our defense against the other side's contentions.

ASSISTANT: Do you plan to make exhibits of any of these minutes?

COUNSEL: Perhaps. Bur first I also want you to analyze these minutes from the point of view of other factors. Are they helpful to our point of view or are they detrimental to our point of view? If they are helpful, make two extra copies. Then if I introduce them as evidence there will be copies for the arbitrator and counsel.

ASSISTANT: Can you introduce such minutes in evidence?

Minutes as evidence

COUNSEL: Not always. But if counsel or one of their witnesses makes some statement referring to them, that would give us an opportunity to try to put them in evidence.

ASSISTANT: Suppose the minutes are against our interest?

COUNSEL: Then we won't put them in. I'll try to keep them out if the other side tries to introduce them.

Comment: Minutes, if they are jointly approved and relevant, may be introduced in evidence. But any offers of settlement should be deleted. No offer of settlement or compromise should be introduced at the arbitration hearing. To do so would discourage parties from settling matters during negotiating steps of the grievance procedure. Arbitrators will routinely disregard them if they are offered.

Minutes kept by each party for its own records should not be permitted in evidence. They could, however, be used to refresh recollections of a participant in the meeting.

ASSISTANT: Then about the only exhibits you might have will be these grievance minutes, if you use them, and the agreement.

Use of exhibits

COUNSEL: That's all I can think of right now. But after we develop the case further we might decide on some others. Exhibits can be very persuasive. An imaginative and well thought out exhibit can often be more effective than any other kind of evidence.

Kind of exhibits

Comment: Exhibits should be used to make the point clearly and concisely that the party is attempting to put over. There are many different forms that may be used for exhibits. The exhibits may be narrative. Or they may be diagrams, photos, maps, illustrations, or physical objects. If there is any statistical or financial information it may be presented in the form of charts, bar graphs, or tables. If charts or graphs are used, the figures on which the charts are based should be included on the chart or the chart should be accompanied by a table showing the actual figures.

If the exhibit is used to compare or contrast job duties or practice on a particular subject, the information could be set out in parallel columns with appropriate markings to indicate contrasts or similarities. If the duties of a job are being described, the exhibit may consist of forms used by the employee in the course of his work. Examples of such forms are shipping documents, invoices, inventory records, journals, receipts, and orders. The use of the forms themselves is often much more effective than merely referring to or describing them.

More than one exhibit may properly be put into the record on the same point. If several exhibits are needed to make a point then several should be used. For instance, if a financial problem is involved, one exhibit could be a narrative statement summarizing a balance sheet, another exhibit might be the balance sheet itself, and a third exhibit could be a chart or diagram presentation of certain details contained in the balance sheet.

Source of exhibit   If the exhibit is not the original source of the information, but is computed or constructed from some other source, it should always clearly show the source from which it was derived. The sources should be made available to the other side for its examination of them. And, it is extremely important that the computation or compilation be accurately made. If the other side is able to show errors in the exhibit, it may shake the confidence of the arbitrator in the entire case of the party submitting the faulty exhibit. The exhibit should not contain material quoted out of context. It should not be so constructed that the opposing side could bring in other material from the same source which could change or substantially modify what the party offering the exhibit sought to show.

Exhibits should be so clear, so simple and uninvolved, that they can be presented without lengthy explanation.

Witnesses: interviewing them   COUNSEL: Let's take up the matter of interviewing the witnesses. I want you to make a written record of those interviews. As I told you, the personnel manager came to see me. His story of what happened was hearsay. The actual person who was involved in this grievance was the store manager. We are going to interview him. He's coming into the office tomorrow. I want you to handle that interview.

ASSISTANT: What do you want me to cover in the interview?

COUNSEL: I want you to sit down with him and get from him exactly what happened from the time the clerk came to work to the time she left the store. I want you to know in detail exactly what happened, how it happened, what was said, when, and by whom. Don't assume we know anything at all about the case. Get every bit of information from him that you can.

ASSISTANT: You want me to make notes of that interview?

COUNSEL: Yes, I want you to make detailed notes. When you interview Red, remember that his conversation with Ms. Green, the clerk, is very important. We want to know whether she quit or was discharged and what she said claiming discrimination because she was a woman. We'll have to try and get Red's exact language. A large part of the case may depend on what he said. I want you to do one other thing and I will do it too. "Size up" the manager as he is telling his story.

ASSISTANT: What do you mean, "size him up?"

COUNSEL: Try to determine what kind of witness he will make. Does he look honest? Does he handle himself well? Does he answer questions frankly? In short, let me put it this way: Does he impress you with his testimony?

Witnesses: evaluating them

ASSISTANT: I see. I guess he's called Red because he's redheaded. Is he excitable?

COUNSEL: I want you to test that. Ask him a couple of questions which might get him a little mad. Try to antagonize him and see how he handles himself. In fact, get rough with him. Use your toughest cross-examination technique. We want to know what to expect from him as a witness. We have to anticipate that from the union counsel.

If Red is an excellent witness, the union representative may want to prod or needle him to get him to change his story or show that he's a man who would flare up on occasion. This could give substance to the contention that the woman was discharged and that Red did discriminate against her.

Witnesses: preparing them

ASSISTANT: Let's say we decide to use the witness. Shall we prepare him for the hearing?

COUNSEL: Oh, yes. If we do decide to use him we would certainly want to spend some time preparing him for the hearing. There's nothing wrong, legally or morally, in our determining what the witness will testify to. Unless we do this we have no basis for deciding whether to call him as a witness or not. In fact, unless we do that, we won't know what questions to ask him. That's true of any witnesses we might want to use. Of course, this doesn't mean coaching or telling the witness what to say. That would be legally and morally wrong. After we question the witness and decide that we want to use him, we should list the questions we intend to ask the witness in writing. By that time we should know what to expect as answers. The witness should be pretty familiar with the ground we will cover in the direct examination. If we can figure out what questions the opposing party is likely to ask on cross-examination, we might let the witness know what to expect. We certainly want him to tell the truth. But we want to avoid the kind of surprise question that might throw him into confusion.

Instructions to witnesses

Comment: Witnesses should be instructed to answer all questions in a concise and straightforward manner. They should be told only to answer the questions asked of them—they must avoid volunteering information not required by the question. And they should be warned not to get into arguments with their cross-examiner. Sometimes counsel will ask a witness during cross-examination if he discussed his testimony with anyone. Many laymen have a mistaken notion that such a discussion is not proper. They freeze up, or hesitate, and often reply that they did not have such a discussion, when it is clear that their counsel must have talked to them in order to know what questions to ask on direct examination. The witness' guilty attitude, when in fact he is not guilty of any misconduct, may partially destroy his credibility as a witness. He should be told to reply to any such question in the affirmative. If he is then asked what he was told to say, he should respond that he was told to tell the truth, since that is what he should have been told.

————

ASSISTANT: Do you think there will be any other possible witnesses to interview besides Red?

COUNSEL: Yes. There is a detective agency report involved in this case. Apparently our client has a detective agency that sends shoppers around to see that sales are properly rung up, whether there is any improper handling of cash, and matters like that.

There was a shopper who went to the store and reported that this clerk did not give the customers sales slips. Now, the personnel manager didn't mention it, but I know in one of our former cases there was a store rule with respect to the handling and wrapping of sales. If I remember correctly, that rule provided that at the time of any sale the customer must be given the sales slip and each sale must be rung up.

Company rules   ASSISTANT: Where was this rule? Do we have a copy?

COUNSEL: No, we don't. We're not sure if Ms. Green has seen a copy of these rules, or whether they were properly posted. The personnel manager didn't raise the point. This sort of thing often happens.

Employers might not mention things like this because they think they are immaterial. But they might be very material and important. Certainly in this case we want a copy of the store rules.

ASSISTANT: Where do I get that?

COUNSEL: From the manager of the store.

ASSISTANT: Is it in writing?

COUNSEL: I assume so. Be sure you have the copy of the rules in effect at the time of the incident. We don't want to start using the rules and then find out that they aren't the right ones.

ASSISTANT: All right. I'll make a note of that.

Subpoenas

COUNSEL: We may need to have the detective agency official who wrote the report testify. But he may not want to; they like to retain their anonymity. But without him I don't think we can get the agency report in. I'm sure the other side will want to cross-examine him.

ASSISTANT: How can we get him if he doesn't want to come?

COUNSEL: We can subpoena him. Our state law authorizes it and even if it didn't, I'm pretty sure, since this matter is in the private sector under federal labor law, that the federal courts would support a subpoena as well. But, since the agency does a lot of work for our client, we better check with him first; he may not want to testify even though it weakens our chances.

Subpoena of witnesses and documents

Comment: The authority to subpoena witnesses to testify, as well as to subpoena documents, is granted under many state laws and has been upheld in federal court in private sector cases.

The party seeking a subpoena must have the arbitrator sign it and the party must serve it by having it presented in person to the individual to be subpoenaed. The geographical scope of the subpoena must be considered as well. There also may be specific requirements such as posting a specified sum of money with the arbitrator to subpoena a law enforcement officer. Subpoenas duces tecum are subpoenas for documents. They are often used to secure medical records, for example, or other documents which may be relevant to the case. Subpoenas should be obtained well in advance of the hearing so they can be served to avoid delay in the hearing date. Since subpoenas duces tecum are generally only to secure documents, they should specify that the holder of those documents does not have to appear if the documents are delivered by a date specified in advance of the hearing. In this way the documents can be studied and copies made for exhibits also well before the hearing.

Arbitrators will probably routinely sign subpoenas provided that they do not appear to be overly broad on their face.

It should be noted that arbitrators do not have any authority to enforce subpoenas by contempt as courts do. If a subpoena is not observed, the party who obtained it may ask the arbitrator to draw adverse inferences due to nonproduction if the nonproducer is the opposing party in the proceedings. Otherwise the party seeking the attendance of a nonappearing subpoenaed witness who has been served but does not attend, where his or her testimony is not stipulated to, can seek a recess of the arbitration and move to the courts to enforce the subpoena. (Subpoena forms are set forth in Appendix C.)

Posted rules

COUNSEL: I want you to ask Red exactly how the store rules were handled, where they were posted, were they readable, were they available for inspection by the employees, and particularly by this employee. I also want you to find out under what authority they were issued and posted, or was there anything in the agreement that prohibited them from being posted.

ASSISTANT: You said something about the rules being "readable." What do you mean?

COUNSEL: I had a case where the company claimed they discharged a machinist for violation of a company rule. The rules had been posted. It looked like the company had a cinch case. But the union proved that the machinist did not know the rule. And the arbitrator decided in favor of the union.

ASSISTANT: But I thought you said the rules were posted?

COUNSEL: Yes, but the copy posted was in small type—it had been dittoed and had faded. It would not have been reasonable to expect anyone to know that these were house rules, or to be able to read them if they did know there were such rules. It always seemed to me that if house rules were important enough to be issued, they should be printed in large legible type on cardboard cards no less than 12" by 14", and then placed in a number of strategic locations in the plant, office, or store.

ASSISTANT: You'd think employers would want to make them easy to find and read.

Counsel: In some plants it might be a good idea to post copies of the rules translated into languages other than English where the makeup of the work force makes this advisable. The main point is to communicate the house rules to all employees who might be adversely affected if they should violate them. You can't justify punishing employees for breaking a rule they didn't know existed. That means we need to cross-examine Red to find out if those rules have been enforced. If enforcement had lapsed, were employees told they would be enforced again? If not, we may be out of luck on that one.

Assistant: What about the detective agency? What do you want me to do about that?

Counsel: Apparently it was a shopper from the detective agency who reported that this clerk did not give him a sales slip. We may have to use this shopper as one of our witnesses, and he should be interviewed as soon as possible.

Assistant: What do you want me to get from him?

Counsel: I want you to find out exactly what happened from the time he entered the store to the time he left. Get his complete story.

Cross-examine him just the way you will Red. You will probably find that he made a written memorandum of what occurred. The report, as I understand it, is a typed report probably prepared in the detective agency's office from his notes. I want you to be able to trace what happened in the store; follow it through to his memorandum to the agency and then to the final report that came to the store manager from the agency.

If the final report was prepared by the head of the detective agency then I want you to interview him as to how he prepared the final report, and his basis for it. The report is what we are relying upon, not the shopper's notes.

Assistant: Why is all of this work necessary? You're not going to use all these witnesses, are you?

Counsel: It is impossible to be overprepared. The greater the preparation the better position we're in to put on a good case and defend against the other side, and it helps us analyze our own weaknesses and prepare defenses for them.

Personnel file

Now, one other thing I want you to get from the store manager is this clerk's personnel record. That starts from the date of her employment with the store chain. I want you to analyze that record carefully, and I want it in our office so that I can analyze it, too. We want to find out just what type of person we're dealing with. And we want to know as much as we can about her record with the company.

ASSISTANT: All right. Now, what about the sick leave pay complaint? Is there anything special to do on that?

Type of dispute

COUNSEL: Be sure to remember that issue when you're analyzing the agreement and checking for changes in preceding agreements. That looks like what we call a straight "agreement interpretation" problem.

ASSISTANT: Aren't they both agreement interpretation issues?

COUNSEL: In a sense, yes. But in the discharge issue there appears to be a dispute on the facts—what were the clerk's actions, what did she mean by her actions, and then how does the agreement apply to the facts. In the sick pay issue, on the other hand, I think we will find that we all agree on the facts, but we don't agree on the meaning of the agreement language.

ASSISTANT: I see the difference.

Investigate setting of dispute

COUNSEL: There is one other investigation we should make. If the clerk quit or whatever happened, it took place in the back room of the store, in the store manager's office, I think. We should view the premises.

ASSISTANT: Do you want me to go to the store and take a look at the store and the back room?

COUNSEL: Yes, before you interview the witnesses. I want you to go to the store and see the physical setup. I will probably go with you. I want to see it, too.

ASSISTANT: Do you usually make such visits?

COUNSEL: Yes, always, because it's invaluable in preparing and examining witnesses. I can visualize all the testimony more clearly.

ASSISTANT: Do you think it might be of some help to draw a diagram that maybe you would want to use in the case, showing the location of the door and the check stand and the back room?

COUNSEL: I'd like to have that very much. We are going to have to illustrate the physical setup of this store and explain what occurred, where the clerk went, how she walked out. It may be very helpful in presenting the case to the arbitrator. The arbitrator may want to see the store but if not, we want to illustrate and explain to the arbitrator where the various incidents occurred.

Diagrams and photographs

Comment: Where reference is made to the scene of an incident pertinent to the case, diagrams or photographs of such areas should be made available in the hearing. It is far easier to understand the evidence with the aid of such diagrams or photographs. It may be desirable to have the arbitrator actually visit the areas in question.

In cases where it is necessary to describe operations or machines, it could be best to have the arbitrator view such operations or machines. Viewing the operations or machines should precede any testimony that may be offered relative to the operations or machines. The arbitrator can then more easily follow the testimony, particularly if it is technical in nature.

ASSISTANT: What's going to be our theory of the "discharge-quit" issue?

Theory of case

COUNSEL: There are still a few holes in our facts, but I think we can develop a theory of our case. For instance, we must check the information very carefully to find out if she ever said to the store manager, "I quit." If she did, we're in a pretty good position. If she didn't, then we have to know exactly what she did say when she left the store in a huff. I think we may find that an atmosphere developed during the discussion that made it reasonable for Red, the store manager, to assume that when the clerk picked up her coat and walked out she was quitting. If Red assumed she quit, we want to present fully the reasonable basis for that assumption.

ASSISTANT: What if we can't persuade the arbitrator that Red was reasonable in assuming that she quit?

COUNSEL: We're going to develop sort of a double shot approach. First, we will argue that she quit, or acted in such a way as to lead Red to reasonably believe she quit. But we'll also argue that if she didn't quit she was properly discharged. I think we'll find that Red's statements on the day after the argument could be interpreted as a discharge. This part of the case will be built around the detective agency report and the store rules. We'll assert that by failing to observe the store rule requiring the clerk to give the shopper a register slip, there was proper cause for discharge.

In any case, we are going to be limited by the reasons that the employer used as a basis for discharge at the time of discharge. We can't support our claim with any reasons Red might have thought up later.

ASSISTANT: So our theory of the case will be that the clerk quit, but that if she didn't quit she should be considered as having been discharged for proper cause because of her failure to comply with store rules.

What about the claim of discrimination?

COUNSEL: We will have to hear the union's case on this question. In the meantime, check Red's conversation with her to see if any discrimination can be concluded from what he said. Also, check on their past relationships; whether she had been given any promotions in the past.

Other arbitration awards

COUNSEL: Right. We should also take one other step. I want you to search for arbitration awards covering similar factual situations. Find out how other arbitrators have ruled. You may not find exactly similar facts, but if they're close enough to raise the same issues study them carefully. Those awards may not influence the arbitrator, but at least they might give us some theories, some arguments, and some ideas that have been used in other cases.

ASSISTANT: Even if we find some favorable rulings, they would never convince the union that we're right on the dispute.

COUNSEL: Don't forget that we're not trying to convince the union. We have a judge up in front of us at the hearing; the arbitrator is our judge. He's the one we have to convince. Remember, the arbitrator is the key person, and we should keep him in mind every minute while we're preparing the case. It's true that other awards are not binding on the arbitrator. But they might help to persuade him or her that either or both of our theories of the case are not out of line, and should be adopted by him or her.

Evaluation of case   ASSISTANT: What happens after we finish our preparation and we conclude our chances are weak?

COUNSEL: This is, of course, one of the very important purposes of thorough preparation. We are advocates, we aren't mere soldiers. We have the obligation to represent our client as well as we can. That means to let him know our candid view of the situation. We may have a loser—maybe Red dressed up the situation to the Personnel Manager to avoid being seen in a bad light. Or maybe we discover other adverse things along the way.

Part of our responsibility—what we're being paid for—is to tell the client this. We must evaluate the case from two aspects: First, whether we think we can win; and second, even if we can, should we pursue the case. The second is touchy and is for the client to decide. But we've had a lot of experience, and if trying the case will open such deep wounds with the client's continuing relationship with the union, either at the store level or between the company and the union, we sure should let the client know our views. It's the old "win the battle but lose the war" problem. We've had an awful lot of experience, and sometimes we have to explore this in depth with the client to disclose the long-range as well as the short-range impact of the case with him. If we conclude that the case looks tough to win we also have to tell the client that. He needs to know this to justify whether to spend the money on a loser.

Also, if back pay is due we may not want to wait for the decision but we may want to cut our losses quickly. With our client's permission, we then ought to get into settlement negotiations quickly to end this matter as soon as we can.

We should do the same if we've got a sure winner. We should let the other side know what we've got and try to talk them out of taking the case, although sometimes they may not be able to back off but would rather let the arbitrator make that decision rather than settle. I don't like that but I think it is better for our long-run relationship to have the integrity and the guts to own up to what we have or don't have by way of a winner or loser.

Furthermore, even if we should win from the arbitrator, this would not prevent Ms. Green from pursuing a Title VII complaint on her claim of discrimination. A court does not have to defer to the arbitrator's decision. Thus, Ms. Green could get "two bites" of the apple. And this would mean more expense for our client.

Now that I think of it, even if our chances are so-so, we should still try to settle. We don't know how the arbitrator will go, and can't predict it too well. So I'd like to keep control over our own destiny by settling rather than shooting the dice with the arbitrator, no matter how experienced he or she may be.

Checklist:
Preparation of the Case

The conversation between the counsel and his assistant illustrates the steps which must be taken to adequately prepare an arbitration case. The steps include:

1. Analyze the present agreement: This involves ascertaining the pertinent provisions relating to the dispute, studying the agreement as a whole, and applying the provision to the facts in question.

2. Study preceding agreements: The history of the pertinent provisions should be studied to see whether or not any changes have been made. There is an advantage, too, in making such a study for the purpose of discovering other cases that have either been settled under the specific provision of the agreement by the parties themselves or cases that have gone to arbitration.

3. Study the grievance committee minutes and other documents presented or used by the grievance committee: Such a study can be extremely profitable. It will disclose the respective positions of the parties. It may actually disclose the theory of the case upon which the other party is relying. In any case it gives to an outsider, such as the counsel, or anyone else presenting the case, the background of the dispute.

This background is invaluable in presenting the arbitration case. It is quite clear that the more familiar an advocate becomes with his case, the more intelligently he can present it.

4. Interview witnesses and make a detailed written record of the interview: This interview should be distinguished from the direct examination that is conducted at the hearing if the witness is used. The detailed interview is primarily for the information of the counsel. Based upon the interview, counsel will determine (1) whether to use the individual as a witness, and (2) what the nature of his or her direct testimony will be. It is a good practice if counsel determines to use the individual as a witness, to set forth in broad outline the general questions which counsel intends to put to the witness upon direct examination. Interviewing a witness is not only useful to obtain the facts, but also to size up the witness, to try to evaluate what kind of an impression the witness will make upon the arbitrator. Is he a witness who will transfer his testimony and evidence with sincerity to the arbitrator? Is he a witness who will stand up under cross-examination, or, even though telling the truth, is he liable to "blow his top," so that the overall impression of the witness' good testimony will be lost?

5. Secure any pertinent documents: In this particular case, this means getting the store rules; studying them; ascertaining their history; finding out when and where they were posted; whether they were "readable;" finding out whether the store rules have any relationship to the written collective bargaining agreement.

6. Intensively study the claimant's personnel record: This allows counsel to become familiar with anything that the personnel record may disclose about the employee's character, work record, personality, and other information concerning her.

7. Visit and view the scene of the dispute: This preparation can be of great value to counsel. As counsel pointed out to his assistant, he is better able to visualize the testimony if he can see where the events were supposed to have occurred. And in so doing, he may be more successful in transmitting to the arbitrator his particular point of view in his presentation of the arbitration case. A diagram may prove very helpful. In many cases, such diagrams or even photographs should be introduced at the arbitration proceeding so that the arbitrator will be aided in visualizing the actual scene of the dispute. And, of course, as is done in many cases, it might be valuable to have the arbitrator visit the scene of the dispute if such a visitation will materially aid in presenting the case to him.

8. Prepare the witnesses: The parties should decide what witnesses will be used at the hearing. These witnesses should be prepared by going over the subject matter and by being told what questions will be asked in direct examination, and what questions they might expect in cross-examination.

9. Decide upon and prepare the exhibits: Exhibits form an important part of the record. They should be approached imaginatively with due recognition of their persuasive value. And they should be prepared thoughtfully and carefully.

10. Develop the theory of the case: It will be noted that counsel expects to be able to develop a theory of the case from this detailed preparation. He has already done so on a preliminary basis from his preliminary investigation. But now he has to make a final determination of how he intends to proceed. He must select his theory so that all the evidence will be pointed toward supporting his theory and all the evidence he can get in his favor will constitute a defense to the theory of the other side. Therefore, he must not only develop a theory of his own case, but attempt to ascertain the theory of the opposition.

In this particular arbitration, it is quite clear what the opposition theory will be. Namely, that the employee was discharged and did not quit; the employer's theory is that she quit and was not discharged. And the union in any case will argue sex discrimination.

And in order to bolster the theory that Ms. Green quit, the employer will seek to rely upon the fact that she quit because she walked off the job. Then the employer will develop what can be called a secondary theory: That if the arbitrator accepts the position that she did not quit, that then she was discharged for proper cause; that cause being violation of store rules by failing to put the cash register tapes in the packages. And this latter theory rests on the store rules, their alleged violation, and the evidence supplied to the store by the Detective Company.

Chapter VII
Arranging for the Arbitration

The process of arranging for an arbitration includes a number of housekeeping details which are important and should not be overlooked by anyone who is preparing for an arbitration hearing.

The following telephone conversation between an arbitrator and counsel will illustrate some of the housekeeping matters involved in an arbitration:

Notifying arbitrator of his appointment

COUNSEL: As you know, I represent the X Union.

ARBITRATOR: Yes.

COUNSEL: The union has a dispute with the Z Company which is now going to arbitration. The attorney for the employer and I adopted the procedure of exchanging a list of arbitrators, five from each, and your name appeared on both lists. As a result of that we have agreed mutually on you as the arbitrator for this case.

Employer's counsel has asked me to call you to tell you of your appointment and to discuss the procedure for the hearing.

ARBITRATOR: Thank you very much. Just for my records, after our conversation I'd appreciate a letter from both you and the employer's counsel noting my appointment. Have you agreed to a submission agreement?

COUNSEL: Yes. We'll send it along with your notice of appointment.

Comment: Presently most parties do not provide "submission agreements." Appendix D describes such an agree-

68

ment, how it is arrived at, and the negotiation of which could provide another opportunity to settle the grievance without going to arbitration.

ARBITRATOR: What about prehearing briefs?

COUNSEL: We prefer not to file any.

Comment: On rare occasions the parties want to file prehearing briefs. These are actually written opening statements. If the parties have stipulated to some facts, they may include these in the briefs. In practice, when prehearing briefs are filed, the parties nevertheless may cover much of the same ground in their oral presentation.

ARBITRATOR: Where are you going to have the hearing?

COUNSEL: We haven't done anything about that. What's your suggestion?

Hearing room

ARBITRATOR: Well, the last time I was in an arbitration (not with you, gentlemen), we had a room that was very bad for a hearing. The light wasn't good, the ventilation was bad, and it filled up with smoke very rapidly.

Please get a room that is well lighted and well ventilated. People get pretty tired as the hearing progresses and if the physical surroundings aren't reasonably comfortable, they become irritable and many times we have arguments in the arbitration hearing we ought not to have.

Then, make arrangements for drinking water and glasses, and some writing pads and pencils.

Arrange enough legible copies of exhibits

Then there is one other thing, and again I'm just pointing this out as a matter of form, as I do whenever I'm selected, if there are going to be exhibits in the case—and I assume there will be, won't there?

COUNSEL: I believe there probably will be.

ARBITRATOR: Can you make it a point, and also ask counsel for the other party to have enough copies of exhibits so that I will get a copy and each counsel will have a copy. And the copies should be readable. I've had some copies that were so badly duplicated that nobody could have read them.

COUNSEL: We'll be sure to take care of that.

Comment: If counsel knows he is going to use a large number of exhibits, he or she could prepare them punched for loose-leaf ring, hard cover binders. Binders should be supplied to the arbitrator and opposition counsel. This provides a neat and orderly method of preserving the exhibits as they are presented. It adds a precision to the presentation of the case and assures that the arbitrator will have all of the exhibits in one place, making them readily available and easy to work with.

Use of a reporter

ARBITRATOR: Have you discussed employing a reporter?

COUNSEL: Well, I know from past cases, you always like to have a reporter. However, I don't like to tell you this, but in this particular case my client hasn't had many of these arbitrations, and they do not want a reporter. They are trying to save money. I'm having a little difficulty getting over to them the real need for a reporter. Maybe you can help me on that.

ARBITRATOR: I assume they want this case decided on what you and I would call the record?

COUNSEL: That's correct.

ARBITRATOR: All right. Now, I think you ought to point out to them and make it clear that there are only two ways to have a complete record of the case: Either the matter is submitted completely on briefs, and counsel can do that if you want to, or if we are going to have hearings, then there should be a transcript of the entire proceeding.

Tell them that if they expect me to sit at the hearing and make notes, I won't have a chance to listen too closely to the testimony. I'm no shorthand reporter and I can't make notes of everything that's said. And as you know, something might be said in the afternoon of a day's hearing that is important only if I know what was said on the same point in the morning of the hearing, and that may be the one item that I did not record in my notes.

COUNSEL: That's a good point.

ARBITRATOR: You see what I mean. If I'm taking it down in longhand, how would I know what to select to take down, until after I've heard the whole case? So, you tell them that as a matter of practice I prefer them to have a reporter, but if they think it's too expensive, let them submit the whole matter on briefs.

The advocates, in a case without other witnesses, may themselves testify to certain matters within their knowledge. This fact, in addition to the fact that the oral arguments of the advocates should be a part of the record, makes a reporter desirable.

Of course, I don't know anything about the case, but if there is any further litigation it will be helpful to a court to have a record of what went on in the hearing.

COUNSEL: Thanks. I think we can work this out.

ARBITRATOR: There's still another advantage to a transcript: The existence of a written record—a transcript or briefs—is a very important incentive to make arbitrators stay with the record when they come to write their opinion and decision. I've also found the parties stick to the case when it's been reported, they don't stray as much from what's relevant.

COUNSEL: That is an important use of the transcript.

ARBITRATOR: And the transcript is insurance for the arbitrator—if some party claims that certain matters were not placed in evidence—or if they question some of the testimony.

COUNSEL: What about the time for the hearing?

Date of hearing

ARBITRATOR: Let me give you two or three dates and we will pick out a mutually agreeable one for the hearing.

Do you have a feeling for how long the hearing might last?

COUNSEL: I think a day of hearing will do it.

ARBITRATOR: OK, I'll give you my first available dates.

Comment: Given crowded calendars of arbitrators and parties, counsel should attempt to accurately estimate the length of the hearing. And, dates should not be confirmed *until after* counsel has checked to see that all his or her witnesses are available on that date.

Checklist:
Arranging the Hearing

As mentioned in the foregoing conversation, the housekeeping arrangements for an arbitration include the following:

1. Sending proper notification to the arbitrator.

2. Sending to the arbitrator the submission agreement if the parties have agreed on the submission, and the prehearing briefs (if the parties have decided to use them).

3. Selecting suitable hearing rooms.

4. Arranging for enough copies of exhibits.

5. Arranging for the use of a reporter.

6. Estimating the length of the hearing.

7. Setting the date for the hearing.

Chapter VIII
The Issue for Arbitration

An arbitrator's authority is reflected in the specific issue or issues agreed to by the parties and submitted for decision. If an arbitrator exceeds his jurisdiction, that is, makes an award not encompassed in the issue, the award can be vacated or nullified by court action. Agreement provisions provide or should provide that the arbitrator does not have the authority to amend, add to, or subtract from any of the provisions of the agreement.

Therefore, agreeing upon the issue or issues to be submitted to the arbitrator is of prime importance. And the relief sought by the complaining party should be stated. Note the following discussion between the employer and union representatives.

Issues to be submitted   EMPLOYER: Now, we'd better get down to one of the important items, the issue, the question to be submitted to the arbitrator. We want to clearly define his authority.

And I guess we've all found that too little time is spent on the wording of the precise question. With that in mind, I have worked very carefully on a question that I think is entirely fair. May I submit this to you as the question we will present to the arbitrator?

UNION: Yes, surely.

EMPLOYER: (1) "Was Ms. Green justified in quitting her employment?" (2) "Was Ms. Green discharged for proper cause?"

UNION: I appreciate the care with which you have considered these questions. But I hope you didn't expect to win the arbitration before it even starts by the form of the issue you propose. The basic issue here, so

73

far as the union is concerned, is that the clerk didn't quit at all. Rather, we claim that she was discharged improperly under the terms of the agreement. So you're asking me by your proposed question to admit in advance that she quit. I couldn't accept that kind of a question.

EMPLOYER: I see what you mean. First, on the question whether the clerk quit or was discharged—would you agree with a statement such as this: Did Ms. Green quit or was she discharged? That's what we want the arbitrator to decide, isn't it?

UNION: Not quite. He could decide that she was discharged but we still wouldn't know whether we could insist on your putting her back to work. We're claiming she was discharged in violation of the terms of the agreement.

EMPLOYER: Well, of course, our position goes further, too. We claim that if she was discharged, she was discharged properly for violation of store rules.

UNION: I know you're going to argue that.

There are two ways, as you know, that we can set up the issues. We can set forth the respective issue proposals of each of the parties and ask the arbitrator to determine which issues are correct after he has heard the case. Probably that procedure would work in this case.

Let's try this one: "Did Ms. Green quit her employment and, if not, did her discharge violate the agreement?" That will give you a chance to argue that she quit and both of us a chance to argue as to whether any discharge was proper.

As to relief, if the arbitrator rules that Ms. Green was discharged in violation of the agreement, the union will request that she be reinstated with full rights as to seniority and back pay from the last date of her employment. That is the question we want answered and it permits each of us to present our respective contentions.

EMPLOYER: That seems like a fair statement.

UNION: All right. Now let's consider the sick leave question. As I said before, we're not claiming that Ms. Green was absent for four working days because of illness. We're arguing that the sick leave clause in the agreement doesn't require that the minimum of three days be working days. It just says "days" and we think that means calendar days. She was sick four calendar days.

EMPLOYER: I don't see how she can claim anything if you don't argue she was out for at least three working days. Nobody would think the agreement means anything else.

UNION: Well, we think the provision means calendar days and we're going to argue that to the arbitrator. And we want the statement of the issue broad enough so that we can argue that way. Why don't we just state it, "Is Ms. Green entitled to sick leave pay?"

EMPLOYER: That's not specific enough. We should include the exact dates which we are arguing about. After all, this isn't an abstract question. In this case, we're really asking the arbitrator to decide how to interpret the agreement provision. How about this? What shall be the application of Article 12 of the Agreement dated April 1, 1985, as this paragraph pertains to the "three-day period?" Shall the application be "calendar days" as contended by the union or working days contended by the employer? That way, we'll have the question completely settled.

UNION: That's all right with me. Well, I think we understand each other on the issues. From my notes, let me dictate the agreement right now to my secretary while you are here.

Test as to issue statement

Comment: The disagreement on how to state the issue may arise because one party or the other is insisting upon a "loaded" statement of the issue. For example: "Was there just cause to discharge John Jones after he hit the foreman who swore at him and pushed him?" This statement includes the position of one of the parties. It assumes facts and makes conclusions. In short, it not only includes the question to be decided but it also includes a statement of the position of one of the parties.

There is a single test to apply to separate out the issue from contentions of the parties. The test is: What question or questions do you want the arbitrator to answer? In the example given, the question to be answered by the arbitrator is: "Was John Jones discharged for just cause?"

The statement that the foreman swore and pushed Jones is what the union apparently intends to argue as an excuse for Jones. But this position of the union and the contentions of the company, whatever they may be, are what will have to be placed in evidence at the hearing. And it is the arbitrator's function to weigh this evidence in order to determine whether or not there was just cause for the discharge.

Therefore, the statement of the issue must be an objective statement; a statement that does not include as a conclusion the claim, or part of the claim, made by either party. If the parties cannot agree on a statement of the issue, the arbitrator can sometimes assist the parties to state the issue. Because the wording of the issue submitted to the arbitrator goes to the very heart of his jurisdiction and authority, the importance of its being clearly stated cannot be overemphasized.

If the parties are unable to agree upon the issue at the time of arbitration, then each party would state the issue at the hearing, both parties giving the arbitrator the authority to decide which statement of the issue controls in the case after he or she has heard the case on its merits.

The matter of the issue can be agreed to before the arbitration hearing. But often it is not addressed until the parties are before the arbitrator. Then the "negotiation" of the issue should be off the record and only the final agreement of the issue should be placed on the record.

UNION: Was there a letter of discharge in this case?

EMPLOYER: No.

Letters re disciplinary actions

Comment: When an employee is discharged or otherwise disciplined, the employer ordinarily addresses a letter to the employee setting forth the reasons for the action. For example, the letter of discharge in Jones' case stated he was discharged for hitting the supervisor. Suppose at the arbitration hearing the employer seeks to enter evidence concerning Jones' absenteeism record and that he did not report to work in a proper uniform. Such evidence would not be permitted since his discharge was not based on those items.

A grievant is entitled to a clear statement of the basis of the discharge. And he or she can only be expected to defend himself or herself as to those specific charges.

However, in a fight case, even though previous incidents are not identified in the discharge letter, such previous incidents could be considered to establish a "course of conduct" on the part of Jones.

In discharge or suspension cases, employers, to protect themselves, will often identify the specific instance involved that led to its action and add that the discharge is also grounded on the past unacceptable record of the employee. In such cases, evidence pertaining to that record is acceptable. The employer is thus claiming that the final incident was the "straw that broke the camel's back."

Chapter IX

Presenting the Case

The presentation of the case at the hearing is the climax of the arbitration proceeding. All the preparation which occurred at all stages of the dispute, the theories developed by the representatives, the investigations into the facts, were pointed toward their possible use at the arbitration hearing.

The hearing itself is conducted somewhat like an administrative hearing, with the arbitrator presiding. It has, however, more flexibility than a court trial, or administrative hearing, and can be more easily adapted to the type of proceeding which the parties themselves desire or indicate. Thus, it can be legalistic or informal; strictly conducted or free-wheeling. But at all times it should be under control of the arbitrator. He or she should conduct a hearing which is orderly and designed to give both parties a full and fair opportunity to present their cases. With these principles in mind, the hearing should be conducted with dispatch.

The following is the presentation by the union representative and employer representative of the case involving Ms. Green. The parties have submitted one of the issues, the sick leave pay complaint, on written briefs. This presentation is concerned entirely with the other issue: Did Ms. Green quit or was she discharged?

ARBITRATOR: This is an arbitration between X Union and Z Company. This case involves Ms. Ann Green. Are you ready to proceed?

UNION: We are ready.

EMPLOYER: We are ready.

Submission agreement and issue
ARBITRATOR: Joint Exhibit 1 is the issue that both of you have agreed to.

I will read the issue for the record:

"Did Ms. Green quit her employment and, if not, did her discharge violate the Agreement?" The relief

78

sought by the union, if it is found that Ms. Green was discharged in violation of the agreement, is reinstatement with full seniority and back pay to the date of her last day of employment.

————

Comment: Questions have arisen whether "back pay" includes payments for fringe benefits. Requests for relief should clearly ask for such payments.

————

If there is no objection, we will mark the agreement as Joint Exhibit No. 2.

ARBITRATOR: In this case the employer will present its case first.

————

Moving party burden of proof

General Rule

Comment: It will be noted that the arbitrator is asking the employer to open up the case, or as it is usually called, to "move" first. The problem of which party first presents its case must always be distinguished from the problem involved in carrying the burden of proof. Ordinarily, when a complaint is filed, the party who files the complaint is referred to as "the moving party" or the "complainant." And in almost all cases it is the moving party or complainant who proceeds to present his case first to the arbitrator and has the burden of proof in establishing his claim. The other party or the respondent then presents his case, which is in the form of an answer or defense. And at that point the burden shifts to him to prove his answer or defense.

Special cases such as discharge, suspension, promotion

In certain types of cases, however, it becomes clear that the complainant or moving party (in this case the union) should not present its case first. This is so in the instance of discharge or suspension cases. In a discharge or suspension situation, the employer has changed the status quo by terminating or suspending an employee's employment. Presumably, it has done this for some reason, and the basis for such action is within the initial purview of the employer. In an arbitration of a discharge or suspension case, therefore, the employer should move forward first because ordinarily the union is claiming that the reasons advanced for the discharge or suspension are unjust or improper or not in accord with the agreement. Since this is usually the claim of the union, it makes sense to have the employer move first and set forth on the record why it discharged or suspended the employee, that is, the basis for the termination or suspension. Then the union assumes the burden to establish that the reason or basis for the employer's action was not proper or fair.

Unless this order is followed, it is quite likely that the union, if it moved first, may, when putting on its case, set forth what it believes or thinks were the reasons for the discharge or suspension. Then the employer would have to establish that the union's allegations were incorrect. The employer could only do this by actually setting forth why it discharged or suspended the employee in question. The result would be to complicate the record with two cases instead of one.

Therefore, in a discharge or suspension case, the employer should go first. Then it also assumes the burden of proof in its opening case to establish a proper basis, and the evidence supporting such a basis, for the discharge or suspension of the employee in question.

This burden then shifts to the party claiming that the action was unjust, in this case the union, to establish this claim on some relevant basis, that is, that the facts relied upon by the employer were incorrect; that there was no violation of the agreement; that discharge or suspension was an unfair penalty, and so on.

In promotion cases   A similar situation could arise in a case where an employer has, under its agreement provisions, the right to select among contending candidates one of such candidates for a promotion, and the union, under the agreement, has the right to challenge such a judgment. Again, in the interest of an orderly presentation, the employer should move first and assume the burden of proof to establish the proper basis for its selection. And of course the union, if it claims that the basis is improper, unfair, or discriminatory, then has the burden of proving such a claim.

ARBITRATOR: (To employer representative): Do you want to make an opening statement?

Opening statement

EMPLOYER: Yes, Mr. Arbitrator, I want to make an opening statement. I ask you to keep in mind the fact that there are two elements involved in this case: The quit and the discharge.

The agreement before you, which has been offered in evidence as Joint Exhibit No. 2, has within it this provision: Section 15 "The Employer shall have the right to discharge any employee for insubordination, improper conduct. . . ."

There is also involved in this case a store rule, which we will bring forth as evidence. The store rule reads, "All sales people (and Ms. Green was a checker-clerk in a grocery store) must ring up the full amount of each sale and hand to the customer the cash register receipt for such sale."

Bearing in mind the contract provision Section 15 of the agreement, which I have just read to you, and which I am sure you will review—and the store rules, which will come into evidence, the facts are simply these:

Ms. Green was employed as a grocery clerk, working principally on the check stand. The incident in this case involved the check stand. During the morning of June 15, 1985, Mr. Brown, the store manager, told Ms. Green to wash the windows in the front door. Ms. Green, after a discussion at the check stand, rather reluctantly washed the windows, as I believe the evidence will show.

Thereafter, Ms. Green came to Mr. Brown's office and engaged in a conversation with him in which Ms. Green told Mr. Brown that she resented the manner in which he spoke to her in front of customers. Ms. Green also questioned her obligation to wash windows under the terms of the contract, although she had washed the windows. This conversation deteriorated into an argument.

Mr. Brown, the store manager, said, "I also have complaints against you, Ms. Green. You have not been ringing up sales properly, according to our store rule."

Ms. Green got her back up on this. Her exact remarks will be brought out in the testimony, but in effect, she said to Mr. Brown, the store manager, "If you are charging me with being dishonest, I am leaving the store now. You discriminated against me because I am a woman." With that, Ms. Green left the store.

She now claims she was discharged. Mr. Brown, the store manager, alleges that she quit and that he did not discriminate against Ms. Green. In substance, this is the issue. It is very clear; there is no question about it, and I am sure your decision will be in accordance with the facts.

UNION: Mr. Arbitrator, I trust that nothing the employer has said will be considered by you as testimony or evidence. It is so far from the facts—

Opening statement not evidence

ARBITRATOR: I think we all understand that no opening statement is considered evidence or testimony. The opening statement is usually a presentation of what counsel believes will occur.

Does the union wish to make an opening statement?

UNION: Yes. In view of the way the employer has described this case, I think it is necessary at this time for me to make an opening statement. I will try to summarize the facts more accurately so that you will have a better idea of what will be brought out during the hearing.

This is a simple case of an employee with a fine record with her employer, the Z Company, with no adverse marks on her entire employment record. She was employed as a checker in a grocery store for three years.

The manager, Mr. Brown, has been constantly harassing her, attempting to get her to do menial duties, such as washing windows and that kind of thing, knowing all of the time that this employee, highly paid as a checker, should not be required to do that kind of work in the store. This was in fact discrimination because she is a woman.

Nevertheless, she has done the work and, as the employer pointed out, she did wash the windows on this particular day. Apparently, however, Mr. Brown was annoyed at the fact that she did not willingly submit to all of his directions which were made without regard to the terms of the agreement. Therefore, he started an argument with her after she had washed the windows.

In the course of this argument, Mr. Brown made further abusive remarks about her being a woman and her work. Apparently it wasn't enough that he should abuse her, he finally attempted to frighten her by saying, "And I have something else on you. I have a report that you have not been properly ringing up sales." This was said for the first time in this argument. She had no other notice of any dissatisfaction with her work.

This was the final blow, Mr. Arbitrator. As a result of this continuous harassment, this woman, and it is certainly understandable, broke down. She was beside herself, didn't know what to do, she obviously couldn't carry on her work that day, so she simply said "I have got to leave, I am sorry." And she left the store.

The next morning she came back to work at the regular time, and the manager said, "You quit, you don't have a job here any more. I have replaced you."

On the basis of those facts, it is clear that this was a discharge, a discharge without any basis under the terms of our agreement with the store.

Furthermore, we will show that the so-called store rules were never brought to the attention of this employee. She never saw the store rules. Nor was the union aware that there were such store rules, and certainly the rules had never been approved by the union.

Opening statements: Should they be made?

Comment: Generally it would seem to be a good idea to make an opening statement. It provides counsel an opportunity to outline the case, what is intended to be proven, to state the facts and show how they fit into his or her theory of the case. Ordinarily, it is the first opportunity to acquaint the arbitrator with the dispute and the party's theory of it. It is obvious, therefore, that the opening statement should be carefully considered and stated. It should not ramble but should be as succinct as possible while providing the arbitrator with an overview of what is expected to occur.

ARBITRATOR: (To employer representative): Will you proceed now?

Swearing of witnesses

EMPLOYER: A preliminary question, Mr. Arbitrator. In view of the union's opening statement, to which I listened with a great deal of interest and concern, I suggest that we swear all the witnesses today. We want to be certain that we are getting the truth.

UNION: I object to that, Mr. Arbitrator.

Witnesses under oath

ARBITRATOR: There is nothing wrong with putting the witnesses under oath. Either side may ask that this be done, and in many states the arbitrator has the authority to administer the oath. The practice is that if the oath or affirmation is to be administered to the witnesses of one side, it will be administered to the witnesses called by the other side. We will put the witnesses under oath.

Comment: It has been suggested that requiring an oath lends more dignity to the proceeding and thus encourages the parties and their witnesses to conduct themselves in an appropriate manner.

Sequestration of witnesses

UNION: I would like to sequester the witnesses.

ARBITRATOR: Hearing no objection, that will be done.

Comment: In arbitration, normally witnesses will be present in the hearing room unless at the outset of the case one party moves to sequester them by having them leave the hearing room. In that instance, the grievant may remain, even if he or she will be a witness. Also, usually one employer representative will be allowed to stay. Then witnesses are called in one by one to testify. This procedure is often used in cases where witness credibility is crucial to avoid one witness being influenced by other witnesses' testimony.

Persons attending   Also present in the hearing room may be "observers" from one side or both. But arbitration is a private matter between the union and the company, and persons unaffiliated with either side, including members of the press in those rare instances where they seek attendance, may be exluded if one side objects.

Co-counsel   In some situations, personal counsel of the grievant may be present. Since the case is the union's because it arises out of the collective bargaining agreement, such counsel may remain only if the union gives its permission as an "observer." He or she cannot participate unless union counsel joins him or her as the union's co-counsel. If two counsel are present for one side, they normally will be limited to one, rather than both, handling a particular witness or statement. This keeps the proceedings orderly and avoids, as a matter of fairness, "double-teaming" the opposition.

EMPLOYER: Mr. Arbitrator, you said we should move first but there are two elements in this case. We say that Ms. Green quit and therefore was not discharged as the union claims. Now, I know that if this were an admitted discharge the employer would have to "move first," that is, put on our witnesses and introduce our other evidence first.

ARBITRATOR: That's correct.

EMPLOYER: But this isn't an admitted discharge. We claim she quit. Why should we go first in this case?

ARBITRATOR: The original complaint filed by the union claimed that Ms. Green was discharged. Your contention that she quit is in the nature of a defense. We shall treat this as a discharge case. If you claim she was properly discharged, you must prove it; if you claim she quit, you must prove it as a defense to the complaint.

EMPLOYER: Who has the burden of proof?

ARBITRATOR: On the discharge issue, you have the burden of proof. And if you assert Ms. Green quit, you have the burden of proof on that claim, too. The union must then try to show that you didn't prove your case. But if it advances any affirmative argument of its own it has the burden of proof as to such arguments.

Comment: The problem of who moves first was discussed in a previous Comment.

Burden of proof

The burden of proof is the burden of persuading the arbitrator that the action taken was valid and in support of the action taken. This the employer would seek to accomplish in this case.

The union will seek to rebut the contention of the employer. It does not, at this point, have any burden of proof. It simply seeks to establish that the evidence offered by the employer in support of Ms. Green's discharge is not persuasive enough. But if the union advances affirmative arguments against discharge such as claiming discrimination for sex or union activity or any other form of discrimination, or that others were not discharged in similar circumstances, then the union has the burden of proof, that is, the burden to persuade the arbitrator to accept such contentions. Then the employer may seek to rebut these contentions. In short, each party who advances affirmative propositions in support of its position has the burden of proof as to those propositions; the requirement to persuade that its position is correct and supported by adequate evidence.

"Punishment should fit the crime": disparate treatment

In discharge cases the union often may admit the facts upon which the employer has acted. But the union then argues that discharge is too severe a disciplinary action for the alleged "crimes" committed. Stated in terms of a cliche: "The punishment should fit the crime"; or considering the crime, discharge, which is "economic capital punishment" is too severe a punishment. The union, in effect, is suggesting that something less than discharge would be in order. Or the union may argue that the employer in like cases did not discharge or suspend other employees. This is referred to as "disparate treatment."

ARBITRATOR: All right. Proceed.

EMPLOYER: You already have in evidence the agreement, Mr. Arbitrator. I would like to call as my first witness the store manager, Mr. Brown.

ARBITRATOR: All right. The arbitrator has administered the oath. The reporter will note that for the record.

Direct examination

Comment: The purpose of direct examination is to place before the arbitrator by means of questions and answers the evidence which the party hopes will support his contentions.

The direct examination should be organized so as to develop support for the theory of the case upon which the examining party intends to rely. It should be literally "direct." The examiner should have gone over the testimony with the witness so that he will know what questions to ask and what answers to expect. He or she should not repeat questions after having obtained a direct answer to a question. There is no purpose served by repetition. If the examiner wishes to emphasize some fact brought out in the testimony, he or she should reserve that emphasis for the closing argument or summarization to the arbitrator. The direct examination should be used to prove the examiner's own case. Opponent's arguments should not be anticipated by attempting to establish defenses before the arguments are made. There will be an opportunity to answer opponent's case after the opposing party has presented it.

EMPLOYER: Would you please give your full name, Mr. Brown?

BROWN: Red Brown.

EMPLOYER: And for whom do you work, Mr. Brown?

BROWN: I work for the Z Grocery Company.

EMPLOYER: Mr. Brown, this is an informal proceeding, do you mind if I call you Red?

BROWN: No. Everybody calls me Red.

EMPLOYER: All right. Tell us how long you have been working for the Z Company?

BROWN: Oh, let me see. I'd say maybe 15 or 16 years.

EMPLOYER: And what positions have you had in the company?

BROWN: I started first in the warehouse. Then I became a clerk and then I became manager of a store. That's what I do now.

EMPLOYER: At one time, were you a member of this union involved in this case?

BROWN: Yes.

EMPLOYER: And how long have you been a manager of this particular store involved in this incident?

BROWN: I've been there about four and a half years.

EMPLOYER: Now, do you recall the incident that occurred on June 15, 1985, involving Ms. Green?

BROWN: I sure do.

EMPLOYER: Do you recall what time Ms. Green came to work that day?

BROWN: Her shift started at 8:00 o'clock in the morning.

EMPLOYER: Did you see her come to work that day?

BROWN: Oh yes. See, there's only a couple, two or three clerks, except on Saturdays when we have some extras. It's not a big store.

EMPLOYER: Do you recall the first contact you had with Ms. Green that day?

BROWN: It was just the usual thing. You know, she came to work and she was working on the check stand. We've got swinging doors in that store and they get all dirtied up by the kids and I told her to go wash the windows.

EMPLOYER: Now, tell me, what did you say? Can you remember what you said to her? To the best of your recollection use the words you used and the words she used.

BROWN: I told her to go wash the windows.

EMPLOYER: Just that?

Brown: Yes. She knew what I meant. The only ones that ever get washed are those on the doors.

Employer: Did you say, "Go wash the windows" or did you say, "As soon as you finish your duties, Ms. Green, I would like to have you wash the windows on your relief time"?

Brown: There wasn't anything said about relief time. This wasn't during her relief time. This was during her regular time.

Employer: At the time you told Ms. Green to wash the windows were there people waiting to have service from her at the check stand?

Brown: No, no. It was a time when it was slow. Is that what you mean?

Employer: Yes.

Brown: It was slow and we had another checker come on for the relief time. The relief hadn't started yet. So she and one of the other checkers were just standing around, so I said to Ms. Green, "Go wash the windows."

Employer: What did Ms. Green say to you?

Brown: She said she didn't have to do it, she was getting tired of doing it. Because she had done it in the past. And she claimed that the union agreement didn't require her to do it.

Employer: What did you say to that?

Brown: I told her it was none of her business what was in the union agreement. I told her she had to follow my orders and to wash the windows.

Employer: Did you say it in that tone of voice, in that manner?

Brown: Oh, of course not.

Employer: Tell me what you said as well as you remember.

Brown: I said to her very nicely—I said, "Now, look, it doesn't make any difference what's in the union agreement, you go ahead and wash those windows, they're dirty," and she says to me, "That's janitor's work." So, I said, "You wash those windows" and then I walked to the back of the store, because I had to get some cases. Part of my job is to fill the shelves and she came back and she told me—

Employer: Now, just a minute. Did you discuss at all her contention that she wasn't required to do that under the union agreement—

Brown: I told her to go talk to the union about it.

Employer: Just a minute, let me finish my question. Did you explain to Ms. Green in any way if she felt she didn't have to wash the windows she could ask the union to take the grievance up with the employer?

Brown: I didn't tell her that. She's some kind of an officer in the union. She knows those things. Why do I have to worry about that? She was told to wash the windows and that's all there was to it.

Employer: Well, then, as I understand it, following that you went to the back of the store?

Brown: Yes. I went to get some cases and she comes tearing back there and—

Employer: Now, wait just a minute. Between the time you say she "tore" back there and the time you gave her the last instruction to wash the windows and you walked to the back of the store, were the windows washed?

Brown: Yes, she washed the windows. She did do that. She went and washed them. Then when I was back there fooling with the cases, she came back and she was really riled up and still protesting.

Employer: And what was your disposition at that time?

Brown: Oh, I was calm.

Union: I request that all the testimony concerning the windows be disregarded. That incident had nothing to do with the discharge. Anyway, she washed the windows.

Arbitrator: Your objection is accepted.

**Proper
objection**

Comment: Union counsel could have raised an objection to the window incident when the employer first brought it up. And since it was not related to either the quit or discharge it would have been sustained. This would have reduced the size of the transcript.

EMPLOYER: Well, now, who was the first to speak when she came to the back room?

BROWN: Well, she came charging back, like I told you, and I said, "I want to tell you something else, we've had some complaints about you. The boss called me up this morning and told me that you haven't been putting those cash register tags in the packages at your check stand."

EMPLOYER: Now, let me stop you just a minute here. Was that the sole conversation?

BROWN: Oh, that's all I can remember now. These are not exact words, you know. Time has passed, but that's my remembrance. Then I told her, because she was bothering me—the windows had been washed and I didn't want to argue with her any more—so I figured I might as well take the opportunity and tell her about this other thing.

EMPLOYER: And you told her then about not putting the cash register receipts into the packages?

BROWN: That's right.

EMPLOYER: And what did she say to that?

BROWN: Oh, she just got excited and she says, "You're making accusations. You're charging me." I said, "I'm not charging you with nothing. I'm just telling you what the boss told me." Then she got really excited and she got red in the face and she went and grabbed her coat and said, "I can't work here any more today," and out she went.

EMPLOYER: Now, let's stop there. Did she say, "I can't work here any more," or did she just say, "I'm leaving the store"?

BROWN: I can't remember the exact words, but I—I really don't remember the exact words but it was something like that. I know she was very excited. Maybe she did say—maybe she said, "I'm leaving," but all I know is she grabbed her coat and her purse and she just ran out of that place.

EMPLOYER: What were you doing at this time? Were you standing up or were you sitting down?

BROWN: I was standing there. And I didn't know what to do when I saw her do that. After all, you know, she's been there for a long time and we've always gotten along pretty well.

EMPLOYER: What were her final words to you then? I want you to give me those words again to your best recollection now.

BROWN: "I'm leaving the store."

EMPLOYER: All right. Was that the last thing she said to you?

BROWN: That's the last I've seen of her until today.

EMPLOYER: When she picked up her coat and walked out did you say anything to her?

BROWN: I didn't get a chance to. She just walked out.

EMPLOYER: Would it be fair for me to say you were just flabbergasted by her conduct?

UNION: I object to that question. He's putting words in the witness' mouth. Let the witness answer the questions.

EMPLOYER: Did you come to the conclusion, Red, that she had quit her employment?

BROWN: Well, I sure did.

UNION: I will object to that question, too! The arbitrator is the person who will have to decide whether she quit or not.

ARBITRATOR: I sustain the objections.

More on objections

Comment: The making of objections is proper, provided the objections made are not frivolous and have some important point to them. For example, it is well to object if the questioning is "leading" the witness, that is, in effect, stating the answer to the question and simply asking the witness to agree to that answer. Or if the witness is asked for a "conclusion" or "opinion" on the very matter which the arbitrator has the duty to decide. Or if the witness is asked about something clearly irrelevant and immaterial, or had already been asked a question before and answered it.

EMPLOYER: What did you do after that? Did you replace Ms. Green?

BROWN: Yes. I called up the personnel manager and I told him what happened and so he said, "Well, I'll get you somebody else," because I needed somebody right away, and he did.

EMPLOYER: How do you replace employees? Do you know where the employees come from?

BROWN: I don't know those things. I think they get them from the union. I don't know.

EMPLOYER: When the employee came in did you ask whether she was sent from the other store or the union?

BROWN: I really didn't, because—I mean, the personnel manager takes care of that for us in our chain.

EMPLOYER: Now, what was the next contact you had either with Ms. Green or any union representative with respect to this incident?

BROWN: Well, the next morning, Ms. Green came in and reported for work and I told her—"Well, I'm sorry, Ms. Green, we have filled your position. You quit the job yesterday and I called up the boss and he sent somebody over here so I can't put you back on."

Inconsistencies

Comment: Note that just a few minutes before Red testified that he didn't see Ann Green again after she walked out of the store as a result of the argument on the 15th until today, the hearing day. Then he says he saw her the next morning.

Counsel should catch such inconsistencies and resolve them or it may weaken the credibility of the witness.

———

EMPLOYER: What did Ms. Green say, if anything?

BROWN: She said, "I did not quit." And I said, "As far as I'm concerned you did quit. But if you're going to raise an objection you might as well know you were going to be discharged anyway, and you are discharged because you haven't been following the rules of the store about putting register checks in the packages of groceries."

So I said, "It don't make any difference if you want to argue you didn't quit or were discharged, you're out either way."

EMPLOYER: And what happened next with respect to Ms. Green?

BROWN: I don't know. I guess she went to the union. I guess that's why we're here.

EMPLOYER: Did you attend any of the grievance meetings on Ms. Green's quit?

BROWN: No.

EMPLOYER: Do the cash registers used in your store issue a customer's receipt?

BROWN: Yes.

EMPLOYER: What happens to these receipts?

BROWN: The clerk is supposed to place them in the customer's bag.

EMPLOYER: Do the clerks do this?

BROWN: They are supposed to. It's a company rule.

EMPLOYER: Is this a sample of such a receipt?

BROWN: Yes.

EMPLOYER: I offer this sample in evidence as Company Exhibit No. 1.

ARBITRATOR: Any objection?

UNION: No objection.

ARBITRATOR: This sample receipt will be marked as Company Exhibit No. 1. Please give one of the copies to counsel.

Exhibits

Comment: Note that this is a company exhibit. The former exhibits were joint exhibits, which means that they are presented jointly and are a part of the case of both parties. Exhibits that are admitted into the record are evidence. This means that the other side has a right to cross-examine with reference to the exhibits.

Exhibits may consist of original materials such as letters, or joint minutes, or meetings. Or exhibits may consist of copies of documents, such as copies of agreements, copies of personnel records, copies of grievance reports, tables, or charts, computed or compiled from other sources. The sources might be questionnaires, government documents and publications, or court decisions. In such instances the original sources should be noted and should be made available to the opponent to check the accuracy of the computation, summary, or compilation. It is not expected that there is any right to go behind the original sources. Such sources are usually accepted without question. Of course, even though the source is accepted, one may still attack the result. For example, a party may criticize the method employed in constructing the cost of living index or the whole concept of the index, but the particular index for a certain date is not questioned in terms of the accuracy of the computation by the Bureau of Labor Statistics in arriving at the final figure. Before offering several exhibits, counsel should, of course, first consider all of the exhibits in relation to each other to be certain that they cannot be used to contradict each other, in part or in whole. It is conceivable that each exhibit may support the party's case and yet be inconsistent with one another. This tends to destroy their persuasiveness.

EMPLOYER: I show you this document and ask you, is this a copy of the company rules?

BROWN: Yes.

EMPLOYER: I offer this in evidence.

UNION: Wait a minute! I haven't seen these rules. The union has never agreed to them. I don't even know if Ms. Green has even seen them.

EMPLOYER: I'm sorry. I should have first shown you the document. Here it is.

Objections to exhibits

Comment: Exhibits, before being introduced, should first be shown to the other party. It may be that the other party wants to raise an immediate objection to their introduction in evidence, and this opportunity should be accorded him or her. The objection may be overcome if the basis for the introduction of the exhibit—the "foundation" of the document—is presented.

EMPLOYER: I'm not claiming that the union agreed to these rules. They are company rules. Let me ask Mr. Brown a question. Were these rules posted in the store?

BROWN: Yes.

EMPLOYER: Do you know whether Ms. Green saw these rules?

BROWN: I guess so.

UNION: Do you know? Not, do you guess so.

BROWN: I never saw her read them. But she has worked there a long time and she knows that it is a company rule to give the receipts.

EMPLOYER: I offer this in evidence as Company Exhibit No. 2.

UNION: I object. There was no showing that Ms. Green read them.

ARBITRATOR: I will permit this to come in as Company Exhibit No. 2. The objection is overruled. The witness testified that these rules were posted in the store.

EMPLOYER: Now, Mr. Brown, have you seen this document before?

BROWN: Yes.

EMPLOYER: This is an exhibit of Ms. Green's criminal record on moral turpitude. And I will ask Mr. Brown whether he had—

ARBITRATOR: Wait a minute. Are you offering this now?

EMPLOYER: Yes.

UNION: I will object to this, Mr. Arbitrator, as being irrelevant, incompetent, and immaterial, on the traditional grounds.

Use of objections

Comment: The use of objections in an arbitration hearing does not necessarily have the same purpose as their use in a court of law. In a court, counsel uses objections on various grounds (and usually on the classic grounds of irrelevancy, immateriality, and incompetency) to get the judge to rule out offensive evidence on the theory that such excluded evidence will not be heard by the jury and thereby adversely prejudice the members of the jury. Often, of course, the jury will have already heard the ruled-out evidence, and it is quite possible that even though it is officially ruled out it will influence their decision in the case. The most important use of any objection in a court trial is to reserve the right to appeal if the ruling is adverse to the objecting party.

In arbitration hearings, there is no similar purpose for the making of objections. The ordinary rules of evidence do not apply in an arbitration proceeding. And, ordinarily, there is no basis for appeal from an arbitration ruling to another level of arbitration or to a court on the ground that inadmissible evidence was permitted into the record. But objections wisely used do have a place in an arbitration proceeding. The most significant use is to test the question of relevancy if the objector believes the evidence or testimony offered is not relevant to the issue. Objections may also be used to keep the record from being "cluttered up." They may be used as a signal to the arbitrator, when he is studying the record, that in the opinion of the objecting party that particular evidence is either irrelevant entirely or entitled to very little weight.

However, often in arbitration hearings offered evidence is objected to on the ground that it is "irrelevant, incompetent, and immaterial." What is meant is this: Evidence is irrelevant if it does not relate to or bear on the points or facts in issue. It is incompetent if the evidence itself is of the type that is inadmissible, such as hearsay or opinion evidence. It is immaterial if, even relevant and competent, it is of such little significance or importance that it could not aid in resolving the issues.

————

UNION: I object to the exhibit. There is no issue in this arbitration involving Ms. Green's alleged moral turpitude, and I don't know how Mr. Brown knew about this anyway.

EMPLOYER: Mr. Arbitrator, I put this in because the evidence will show that Mr. Brown had this in mind when he discharged her.

UNION: Had what in mind?

EMPLOYER: This moral turpitude.

ARBITRATOR: Just a moment. You said that he had it in mind when "he discharged her."

EMPLOYER: If you would read that, you'd have it in mind, too.

ARBITRATOR: I don't intend to clutter up the record with this huge document unless this is admissible. When Ms. Green was discharged, was she told that this was one of the bases for discharge? Are you making that claim?

EMPLOYER: No. But it was in Mr. Brown's mind.

ARBITRATOR: I would suggest you put it back in your file. It obviously has no place in this hearing. What was in Mr. Brown's mind when he discharged Ms. Green is not relevant. After a discharge, it is not proper to go over the employee's record with a fine-tooth comb and bring up something that the company knew about for a long time but did nothing about. There is no evidence that this record was one of the reasons for the present discharge. This does not constitute a warning which had been properly issued and would now be entitled to weight. It would be most unfair to permit the employer to drag an exhibit into the case raising a question of moral turpitude when it apparently never played a part in the discharge.

EMPLOYER: That's all on Mr. Brown, then.

Evidence in relationship to basis of discharge

Comment: As a general proposition, an employee who has been discharged or suspended is entitled to have his or her case heard on the specific facts used by the employer as the basis for the discharge or suspension. Put another way: Employer A decides to discharge X. He makes up his mind at the time he discharges the employee because of certain facts known or which had been made known to the employee. It is those facts which are placed on the table if the employee decides to appeal the discharge, and the case gets to arbitration. If arbitration results, the employer may not in fairness add at that time other facts or incidents which were not part of the actual basis upon which he formed his final decision to discharge the employee. In fact, the best practice is to give to the employee (and in some cases the union) a written statement of the reasons for the discharge at the time of discharge. If the employer puts the basis for discharge in writing, it will give him a chance to evaluate the fairness of his action. Upon examination, he may find that the reasons do not justify the discharge. He is then in a position to reinstate the employee and avoid costly and unnecessary arbitration.

ARBITRATOR: Cross-examination?

UNION: Yes. I would like to ask Mr. Brown a few questions. Mr. Brown, would you state exactly the words used by Ms. Green when she left the store after the incident on June 15th?

BROWN: She said, "I can't work here any more."

UNION: At another time in this hearing didn't you also testify that Ms. Green simply said, "I'm leaving"?

BROWN: No. I didn't say that. She never said that.

UNION: Well, we will let the record speak for itself. Now, in your conversations with Ms. Green, didn't you say to Ms. Green that you were sick and tired of these "libber" women? And that she was one of them?

BROWN: Absolutely not.

One use of transcript

Comment: A transcript is extremely valuable in this instance. It will be remembered that Mr. Brown testified previously on direct examination that Ms. Green said, "I can't work here any more *today*," and then after further questions concerning the exact words said, he testified that she might have said, "I'm leaving." If Ms. Green said, "I can't work here anymore today," there is a possible inference that she did not quit.

UNION: No further questions, Mr. Arbitrator.

Cross-examination

Comment: Cross-examination refers to the examination of a witness by the other party. Its purpose is to examine the witness upon the evidence given during the direct examination, to test the truth of that evidence, or to further develop it or clarify it.

Although the opportunity to cross-examine witnesses should always be provided, this does not mean that it is always advisable for the opposing party to cross-examine the witness. It has been asserted that the first rule of cross-examination is "Don't cross-examine unless you know the answers to the questions you intend to ask the witness." But there are times when cross-examination is useful, if not crucial. Maybe it appears that the witness is exaggerating or at least skirting around the basic facts, and this should be developed by a few concise questions. There is no doubt that the cross-examining party may materially weaken his case by overusing the tool of cross-examination. Some advocates have a notion that the way to cross-examine is to take the witness over the same ground covered in direct examination. When this is done, it gives the witness the opportunity to restate his or her case all over again, thus further fixing his or her direct testimony in the mind of the arbitrator. By this time the witness may have become more comfortable in his or her role as a witness. And in his or her more relaxed state may suddenly remember more details favorable to his or her side of the case. Or the cross-examination itself may serve to jar a witness' memory adverse to the case of the cross-examiner.

If the opposing party has any doubts about cross-examination, he or she should not cross-examine the witness. It is far better if he or she tries to win the case through his or her own evidence and own witnesses, rather than through adverse witnesses. No one should go into an arbitration hearing depending solely upon the use of adverse witnesses to strengthen or win the case. However, sometimes it may be an advantage in a discharge or suspension case to call the grievant as an adverse witness to pin down that witness' testimony before the party's affirmative case is presented. An adverse witness' testimony is not necessarily binding on the party calling such a witness. Arbitrators may differ on calling discharged or suspended employees as the employer's first witness as an adverse witness, but modern practice appears to allow the calling of anyone by any party as a witness.

ARBITRATOR: (To employer representative): Proceed.

EMPLOYER: My next exhibit ties together the store rules and the cash register receipts that are in evidence with respect to Ms. Green's violation of store rules. It is the report of the Detective Company. We ask that it be marked as the exhibit next in order.

UNION: I will object to that. There has been no proper foundation laid, no indication of where this report comes from, no opportunity to cross-examine the person who prepared the document. It is obviously not admissible.

Comment: This is an example of an exhibit for which the original source is the detective. The source must be produced for the opposing party.

EMPLOYER: Mr. Arbitrator, that report was discussed thoroughly in the grievance meetings. They all know about it.

UNION: Since you mention the grievance meetings, I would like to take this opportunity to offer the minutes of the grievance committee in evidence.

EMPLOYER: I object to the minutes. That is part of our attempt to settle the grievance through negotiation.

ARBITRATOR: Let's take these up one at a time. I need not remind you that we are not in a legal proceeding and are therefore not bound by any of the ordinary so-called legal rules of evidence, even those dealing with the introduction of evidence. Nevertheless, we are bound by several important fundamental principles that apply in arbitration.

Relevancy

One is that evidence offered must have some relevancy to the issue. That is why I ruled out those so-called moral turpitude reports that the employer sought to introduce.

Now, I can see that the report of the Detective Company has relevance to your claim that the grievant violated the rules. But, the other party must also have the right and opportunity to cross-examine the evidence that comes in. Now, you cannot cross-examine the document itself, but you can cross-examine the person or persons who drafted it.

Therefore, I would sustain the objection made by the union on this point. If you want to introduce the report, then you must produce its author. Then the union is in a position to cross-examine. Do you intend to bring in the witness from the Detective Company?

EMPLOYER: I anticipated I might have some trouble on this. My opponent is well known for making things difficult. He seems more interested in prolonging the hearing than in getting at the truth.

Stupid behavior

UNION: Wait a minute! Are you questioning my motives? I don't have to take that sort of thing. I could say a few things about you, for example—

ARBITRATOR: Now, gentlemen, let's remember that this hearing is concerned with issues that have nothing to do with any personal differences both of you may have—real or imagined. This hearing is going to be conducted in an orderly and dignified manner and will be confined to the issues before us.

Comment: This is a mild example of counsel nagging at each other. It should be avoided. Engaging in acrimonious behavior serves no purpose, except to clutter the record and try the patience of the arbitrator, in addition to probably not impressing counsel or constituents. Throughout the hearing, the parties should attempt to develop the confidence of the arbitrator in their role as representatives. In part, this confidence results from his or her observation of the way the parties conduct themselves at the hearing. Any personal exchange between counsel will tend to destroy this confidence, and is, of course, irrelevant to any of the issues before the arbitrator. The attention of the arbitrator should always be kept on the case itself.

———

ARBITRATOR: Let's go back to this question of the Detective Company report. Do you intend putting the detective on the stand?

EMPLOYER: Well, I started to say that I had anticipated trouble in getting this report in, so I took an affidavit from the detective who prepared the report. The affidavit gives the information we need. I wish to offer the affidavit in evidence.

UNION: I object, Mr. Arbitrator. That is not the same thing as having the person here.

Affidavits as evidence

ARBITRATOR: I will sustain that objection. The trouble with letting affidavits and other signed statements into evidence is that it does not allow the opposing party an opportunity for cross-examination or a chance to properly rebut the testimony. I rarely permit such statements to be introduced, unless the opposing party agrees to let them come in. It's true that this is an informal hearing, but a line must be drawn somewhere. We can't make it so informal that the other party is denied the right to cross-examine or rebut the testimony. This could result in a failure of one of the parties obtaining a full and fair hearing.

Will you bring in the detective from the Detective Company?

EMPLOYER: I seem to have no alternative.

Grievance procedure minutes as evidence

ARBITRATOR: We still have the question of whether the minutes of the grievance procedure meetings can come in as evidence.

As a general proposition, I will not permit the minutes of the grievance procedure to come in as evidence because the minutes might contain compromise offers made by the parties in an effort to settle the matter. Compromise offers to settle the dispute should not come into the record. The parties might attempt to settle the matter for many reasons other than on the merits of the case.

Compromise offers as evidence

Therefore, not knowing what is in these minutes, I would not permit them in.

If they are allowed in, they should ordinarily be used to refresh the memory of a witness or to impeach a witness. The minutes themselves are not proof of the facts but only evidence concerning what was said about them.

Shall we proceed?

EMPLOYER: Yes. I will call Mr. Jones from the Detective Company.

ARBITRATOR: He has been sworn.

EMPLOYER: Would you please state your full name?

JONES: Edward Jones.

EMPLOYER: Mr. Jones, is it correct that you work for the Detective Company?

JONES: Yes.

EMPLOYER: And what type of work does the company do and what is your job in the company?

JONES: It engages in several types of detective work. It has several stores as clients. My own work is connected with the stores. My job is to act as a shopper—to go into a store like any other shopper and to find out if the clerks are doing what they are supposed to be doing.

Sort of an outside check to see that clerks are ringing up the sales properly, not overcharging, giving receipts, and that sort of thing.

EMPLOYER: In the course of your work did you have occasion to make a check on the clerks at the Z Store?

JONES: I did.

Employer: In your most recent check at that store, what was the name of the clerk whom you observed?

Jones: Ann Green.

Employer: Would you please look at this report. Have you seen it before?

Jones: Yes. That is the report I prepared on the Z Store and specifically on my observation of Ann Green.

Employer: Mr. Arbitrator, I would now like to offer this report of the Detective Company in evidence.

Arbitrator: Does the union representative have any objections?

Union: No objection.

Arbitrator: It will be marked employer exhibit next in order.

Employer: No further questions.

Arbitrator: (To union counsel): Cross-examination?

Union: Thank you. Mr. Jones, at what time and on what date did you say that you were in the Z Store?

Jones: I didn't say. It's in the report. I was there about 10:00 a.m. on April 10.

Union: How long were you there?

Jones: Oh, about 10 minutes, I guess.

Union: Where were you during those 10 minutes?

Jones: Part of the time I was in the shelving section and part of the time at the check stand.

Union: How long were you at the check stand?

Jones: Long enough to have a bag of groceries rung up. A few minutes.

Union: How did you know that the clerk observed was Ms. Green?

Jones: They only have a couple of clerks there. I had their descriptions from the Personnel Department. It wasn't hard to tell.

UNION: How did you know that this clerk you observed, whoever it might have been, was not putting cash register tapes in the bags?

JONES: She didn't put one in my bag of groceries. You see, we pose as customers, get some groceries, then buy them like anybody else who is shopping, and observe closely to see that sales are rung up, prices are accurate, and receipts given.

UNION: Where were you standing when you were at the check stand?

JONES: Part of the time I was in line, but when the clerk was ringing up my purchases I was standing in front of her, so I could watch her and the cash register.

UNION: Did anyone else see this transaction?

JONES: Well, I don't think so. The store wasn't very busy. There were a few people in front of me, but none behind me.

UNION: As soon as you realized she had not put a receipt in, did you go directly to the store manager, so that he could check the package and verify that there was no receipt?

JONES: We don't do it that way.

UNION: How many other stores did you visit that day?

JONES: About eight.

UNION: Do you stop after each one and write your report on that store?

JONES: No, I usually do all my visits and then go back to the office and write my report from my notes.

UNION: Do you still have your original notes on the Z store, Mr. Jones?

JONES: No.

UNION: How many stores did you visit after the Z Store, before writing your report?

JONES: I don't remember exactly. But from the time I was at the Z Store I would say about five others.

UNION: Isn't it a fact, Mr. Jones, that the companies expect you to file reports that show that your service is worthwhile, that you found something? Isn't it a fact that you are getting paid for being a stool pigeon?

EMPLOYER: Object—I object.

UNION: I withdraw the question. No further questions.

EMPLOYER: Mr. Arbitrator, I offer now in evidence ten arbitration awards that I believe will be pertinent to your consideration of the legitimacy of the employer's position on this matter, and I will ask that they be marked as our next exhibits in order.

UNION: You are offering these in evidence?

EMPLOYER: I am offering these in evidence.

Other arbitration awards

UNION: I will object to this. This is a matter of argument, Mr. Arbitrator, and counsel can put those in a brief if he wants to.

EMPLOYER: I am just trying to help you, Mr. Arbitrator.

ARBITRATOR: I appreciate the help you are trying to give. Are you suggesting that I am bound by those arbitration awards?

EMPLOYER: Having gone over them very carefully, I would suggest that.

UNION: Naturally, he wouldn't pick out any other kind!

ARBITRATOR: Under the agreement am I bound by those awards?

EMPLOYER: No.

ARBITRATOR: You mean they are meant to be persuasive?

EMPLOYER: Very persuasive.

ARBITRATOR: Somewhere along the line you are going to argue this case and at that time you can refer to these arbitration awards. I can assure you I will read them all.

EMPLOYER: But we may reach the stage where we will submit the case without argument or briefs. What am I going to do then?

UNION: I would like to point out that I don't know under what circumstances these awards were made. I don't know the factual circumstances. Obviously they can't be controlling.

ARBITRATOR: They certainly can't be evidence. They are at best what in law practice would be called "points and authorities" in support of your position. They are not evidence.

And if you submit briefs instead of oral argument, you may refer to such awards. I will mark them as employer exhibits for identification only.

Comment: Arbitrators should read awards referred to by counsel. Counsel should read the entire award before offering it. Too often only a part of the award is cited which seems favorable to the case. But a complete reading may disclose material adverse to the case of the party offering the award. The offered decisions could, for the record, be marked as employer exhibits for "identification," which identifies them in the record but not as evidence. The opposing side then may refer to them in its argument and probably should do so if they can be "distinguished" from the case being heard.

ARBITRATOR: You rest?

EMPLOYER: We rest, subject to rebuttal.

ARBITRATOR: Is the union prepared to go ahead?

UNION: Yes.

Before I call my principal witness, Mr. Arbitrator, just so you will understand what this so-called Detective Company report amounts to, I would like to introduce as an exhibit a newspaper clipping which I have here from a newspaper in another city of April 3, 1980, showing where this Detective Company—

EMPLOYER: Just a minute. Just a minute, Mr. Arbitrator.

UNION: I will offer it.

EMPLOYER: Before he characterizes it, I would like to see it. But first I would like to object to it.

ARBITRATOR: Look at it.

EMPLOYER: Even if I look at it I will still object to a newspaper clipping. It is hearsay. It is incompetent, irrelevant, and immaterial. Furthermore—

ARBITRATOR: In the first place, the mere fact that it might be hearsay would not be enough to keep it out. It is clear that the union is seeking to attack the credibility of the Detective Company. For that purpose the evidence might be acceptable. But it relates to 1980; we have no way of knowing whether the branch in the other city is conducted differently from those in this city. We would have no access to any details of the 1980 case. Because of this, the evidence is incompetent or even immaterial. That is, under the circumstances it is not significant enough to aid us in this arbitration. I sustain the objection.

Let's proceed, gentlemen.

UNION: As my first witness, I call Ms. Ann Green.

ARBITRATOR: She has been sworn.

UNION: Would you please give your full name to the reporter?

GREEN: Ann Green.

UNION: What is your occupation, Ms. Green?

GREEN: I'm a grocery clerk.

UNION: How long have you been a grocery clerk?

GREEN: Oh, about ten years, I guess.

UNION: What was your last employment?

GREEN: I worked for the Z Grocery Store. I was a checker there.

UNION: For how long?

GREEN: I guess about four years.

UNION: Have you ever been discharged from any employment?

GREEN: You mean in the grocery business?

UNION: Yes.

GREEN: No.

UNION: Now, would you describe in your own words what happened on June 15.

GREEN: Well, on this day I was doing my usual duties, and Red over there, the manager, came to me and he says, "Go wash those front windows." I had washed them before but every time I washed them I'd tell him I didn't think I should do it, that wasn't my work, that was the janitor's work. But he kept telling me I should wash them. I kept protesting, and he called me a "libber." And then he just ordered me to do it and I told him then I didn't think I had to do it because the union agreement didn't say I had to do it and he told me—and he used pretty threatening language, I thought, the way he said it—in effect, he said, "You better do it." So I washed the windows.

I guess I was pretty boiled up about it, so I figured if I washed the windows—I was going to tell him I wasn't going to—

EMPLOYER: Mr. Arbitrator, I object. If she wants to tell her story, I suggest she tell what was said at the time, not her impressions or ideas or how she felt.

Words used, not "impressions"   ARBITRATOR: Ms. Green, to the best of your ability, try to recall whenever you are talking about conversations the words that you used and the words that the other person used, not your impressions.

GREEN: All right. I'll try.

UNION: All right, proceed, Ms. Green.

GREEN: Well, anyway, I was going back to tell Red, after I washed those windows, that I wasn't going to do it any more until the union told me I had to do it. He was in the back of the store getting some groceries to put on the shelves I guess, and I went back there and was very nice. By that time I was sort of cooled off. But right away he started giving me a bad time again.

Union: What did he say?

Green: Well, this is what he said. He said, "I'm always having trouble with you about washing those windows and I'm getting sick and tired of it. You are one of those 'libbers.' You women think you can run the whole show." Well, that got me excited again and I said, "Look, I washed the windows but I'm going to take it up with the union because I don't think I have to wash them." So he said to me, "Well, go take it up with the union." I was about to turn away to go back to the check stand when he says to me, "And there's one more thing," and I says, "What?" and he says, "I got a complaint from the boss today that you haven't been putting the register tapes in the bags of groceries." And I said, "Are you accusing me of being dishonest?" He said, "I'm just telling you what the boss said."

Well, after I had worked there so long, that just made me sore as the dickens and I just got excited and I said, "Well, I can't continue to work here today" and I grabbed my coat and ran out. I just got excited, that's all. You can imagine, working for somebody for so long and then having him saying that kind of thing about you.

Union: Did you leave the store?

Green: Yes. I left the store.

Union: And that, to the best of your recollection, covers the conversation and the incident that occurred between you and Mr. Brown?

Green: On that day, yes.

Union: On that day. Now, at any time, Ms. Green, did you say to the manager that you were quitting your employment?

Green: No. I wasn't quitting my employment. Why should I quit? I mean, I did my work. They never had any complaints about my work. I did get sore but you would, too, wouldn't you, if somebody made those charges against you? So, I just left, that's all, and the next day at my regular starting time I went back to work.

UNION: You reported to work the next day at your regular time?

GREEN: Yes.

UNION: What occurred that day?

GREEN: Well, Red was there and he said to me, "I can't put you to work" and I says, "Why not?" and he says to me, "Well, you quit," and I says, "I didn't quit," and he says to me, "Well, you certainly did." He said that, "You said yesterday when you left here, 'I'm leaving' or something like that." And I says, "Well, I never said I quit," and Red says, "Well, you better take it up with somebody else because I've got a replacement here already and I can't put you to work."

UNION: Did Red then tell you that you were discharged?

GREEN: He did not! He only repeated over and over again that I quit. Which I didn't.

UNION: Then did you leave?

GREEN: I had to leave. There was no point in standing around. I went to the union.

UNION: You took this up with the union?

GREEN: Yes. I told the union and they said they'd send the business agent to see Red.

UNION: Incidentally, Ms. Green, have you worked since this incident?

GREEN: Well, it took me about two weeks to get a job but I've been working since.

UNION: You were out of work for about two weeks after the incident?

GREEN: That's right. And I couldn't afford it.

UNION: Now, as I understand it, when the manager told you about this, that he had this report that you weren't properly putting the cash register tapes into the bags, you became pretty upset. Did you?

GREEN: Well, sure.

UNION: Why were you upset?

GREEN: Because I always put them in there. I've been working for ten years as a grocery clerk and nobody ever had any complaints about me on that basis and nobody ever complained. Nobody told me I wasn't putting them in. That's like saying I'm cheating or something. That's why I got pretty upset. That's like calling you a thief. He didn't use that word, though.

UNION: But that was the impression you got? I mean, you felt that—

EMPLOYER: Objected to as calling for the opinion and conclusion of the witness. Her impressions make no part of this case.

UNION: I will withdraw the question.

Incidentally, Ms. Green, do you know anything about any store rules in this store?

GREEN: Store rules?

UNION: Written store rules.

GREEN: What do you mean by store rules?

UNION: You remember the rules that Red identified earlier today as store rules?

GREEN: Oh, that. That's the first time I ever heard about store rules. I've never seen any around.

Awareness of company rules

Comment: Arbitrators usually hold that the employer must give evidence that an employee is aware of any company rule upon which the dismissal is based. Some arbitrators have gone further than this and require evidence that the employee knows that a violation of a rule carries the penalty of discharge if discharge is in issue.

UNION: Were you ever warned prior to this incident about putting those tapes into the customers' bags?

GREEN: Well, I wasn't warned. I knew that you have to put them in. That's part of the duties of a clerk.

UNION: Were you ever told you were not doing this properly?

GREEN: No. Nobody ever complained because I always put them in. I know that's what you're supposed to do.

UNION: Had there been any other complaints about your work prior to this occasion except for this running argument that you apparently had with the manager about washing the windows?

GREEN: That's about the only thing I can think of. Otherwise, Red and I got along pretty well. He gets excited sometimes, but—

UNION: He gets excited?

GREEN: Yes. His hair isn't red for nothing.

UNION: All right. That's all.

ARBITRATOR: (To employer counsel): Cross-examination?

EMPLOYER: Ms. Green, you testified that you always put the register tapes in the bags of groceries. Is that correct?

GREEN: Yes, that's right. I always put them in.

EMPLOYER: You can say then, without any doubt in your mind, that every time you made a sale you put the tape in the bag before giving the bag to the customer?

GREEN: Yes.

EMPLOYER: And in every case, you rang up each sale, put the money in the drawer, gave the receipt to the customer, before going on to the next sale?

GREEN: Yes, that's the way we do it.

EMPLOYER: Didn't it ever happen that somebody went by the sales desk with a candy bar or other small purchase and left the exact change for it by the cash register while you were ringing up another sale?

GREEN: The store doesn't like that to happen.

EMPLOYER: Well, has it ever happened to you?

GREEN: Not that I can remember.

EMPLOYER: Ms. Green, if you always put the receipts in the bags, how does it happen that Mr. Jones of the Detective Agency did not get a receipt from you when he made his purchase?

GREEN: I don't understand that. He must be wrong.

EMPLOYER: Now, Ms. Green, you claim that Red discriminated against you because you are a woman?

GREEN: Yes.

EMPLOYER: Is it not a fact that Red certified you to become a journeyman clerk after you served your apprenticeship?

GREEN: Yes.

EMPLOYER: You claim that Red called you a "libber" and isn't it true that you have described yourself as a "libber"?

GREEN: That's true, I am, but Red discriminated against me when he called me a "libber."

EMPLOYER: Now, Ms. Green, you have worked with Red for a long time and isn't it a fact that he has treated you fairly without reference to your being a woman?

GREEN: That's so, except for the present case.

EMPLOYER: No further questions.

Address discrimination claims

Comment: If a charge of discrimination of any kind, color, sex, union activity, etc., is made in the original grievance or develops during the hearing, it should be addressed at the hearing.

UNION: I have a few more questions, Mr. Arbitrator.

Ms. Green, you testified earlier that no one had spoken to you about violating any store rules prior to the discussion you had with Red Brown on the 15th of June. Is that correct?

GREEN: Yes, that's right. That's the first I ever heard any criticism concerning my work. Other than our window-washing disagreement.

UNION: In the four years that you have been at the store, you have never received any warnings about your work?

GREEN: That's right.

UNION: No further questions.

Warnings

Comment: Arbitrators take the view that in certain types of cases an employee should be warned before he or she is discharged. These are instances in which the employee might be guilty of some omission, but the "crime" is not so serious as to warrant discharge. These warnings are intended to give an employee "another chance" and are referred to as "progressive discipline." When warnings are issued, they should always be in writing and, of course, given to the employee, and if the agreement requires, sent to the union. It may be appropriate to send the union copies, in any event. If the warning is the last of several and if it is meant to be the "last chance," it should clearly state this fact. It may be also that a suspension instead of discharge is an appropriate progressive disciplinary step.

There are cases, of course, where the cause of the discharge is so serious, that no previous warnings are required or are in order before resorting to discharge.

ARBITRATOR: Shall we proceed with the next witness?

UNION: I'd like to call the business agent of the union, Mr. Howard Smith.

ARBITRATOR: Mr. Smith has been sworn.

UNION: Would you please state your name and your position in the union?

SMITH: Howard Smith. I am the business agent for the union.

UNION: Is Ms. Ann Green a member of your union?

SMITH: Yes.

UNION: Does your union have an agreement with the Z Company?

SMITH: Yes, we do.

UNION: How long have you had an agreement with it?

SMITH: For about five years.

UNION: Have you been business agent during this entire period?

SMITH: Yes, I have.

UNION: During that period did the Z Company ever discuss with you the so-called store rules which were presented as an exhibit in this case?

SMITH: No.

UNION: Mr. Smith, I want you to take a look at this exhibit, the so-called store rules. Please read it carefully. To your knowledge, has the Z Company ever discussed these rules with the union?

SMITH: No, there has been no discussion on these rules.

UNION: How many negotiations have you had with the Z Company?

SMITH: We've negotiated three agreements.

UNION: During any of these negotiations, were these store rules discussed?

SMITH: No, they were not.

UNION: No further questions.

ARBITRATOR: Cross-examination.

EMPLOYER: No questions.

Comment: The union is laying the groundwork to argue that the company rules are not binding because they were neither agreed to by the union or even discussed with the union. If the union should so argue, the company would probably reply that it has a right to establish company rules under the general authority of management to "run its business." And that such rules are binding, even if not agreed to by the union, so long as the rules do not violate the provisions of the agreement itself.

UNION: We rest.

ARBITRATOR: Is the case now submitted?

EMPLOYER: Yes.

UNION: Yes, as to the testimony and exhibits.

ARBITRATOR: All right.

Now what do you want to do? Do you want to make oral argument or do you want to file written briefs?

EMPLOYER: I am going to request briefs. I would want to analyze the transcript and submit briefs.

UNION: I would be prepared to argue now. But since counsel has asked to file briefs, I will accede to that request.

ARBITRATOR: All right. If you had disagreed on that question I would have had to decide that point. And I would be inclined to grant the request for briefs, since one of the counsel desired to file one.

Closing argument or briefs

Comment: The parties are entitled to oral argument at the end of the submission of their evidence. If the parties prefer, they may waive their right to oral argument and submit at a later time their written briefs. Which procedure is advisable depends upon the nature of the case. If the case is complex and the record is long, some representatives prefer to have an opportunity to review the record before submitting their arguments. Or if the argument involves technical material, written briefs might be preferable to oral argument.

If the parties do decide they wish to present written briefs they should agree upon deadline dates for exchange of the briefs with each other and submission to the arbitrator. And they should agree upon time limits for rebuttal briefs, if any, although a single brief simultaneously filed by each party is normal. If the parties desire the opportunity to examine the transcript, the date for filing briefs is usually stated in terms of so many days after receipt of transcript.

Whether or not the parties argue the case orally or submit their closing arguments in writing, the arguments should have the same general content. It is in the arguments that the parties tie together the evidence submitted during the hearing in such a way as to support their respective positions. It is not simply a summarization of the case. It is a statement of the theory of the case supported by appropriate references to testimony and exhibits that give support and weight to the theory. This is the party's final opportunity to persuade the arbitrator that his or her view of the case is the correct view and the opponent's view is the incorrect view. It should be a carefully thought-out statement. No extraneous material should be included.

The argument should seek to give to the arbitrator such an analysis of the record that he or she could use it to write the opinion and decision if he or she is persuaded to adopt counsel's view of the case. (Additional references to closing briefs are made in Chapter X, Presenting the Case on Written Briefs.)

Bench awards
In some instances a "bench award" may be made by the arbitrator. This type of award occurs in discharge cases or other types of cases where immediate relief may be warranted. In discharge cases, the bench award will be either reinstatement with full back pay or postponing an award on back pay, if any. Bench awards occur only where the arbitrator is so positive as to the outcome of the case that further consideration is not required and where the immediacy of the situation warrants such action to mitigate further damages. Without both such conditions, the arbitrator will want to review the record and arguments before making a decision. And, where bench awards are made, they will be followed by written opinions detailing the basis for the bench award.

Checklist:
Presenting the Case

In presenting the case, the parties should keep in mind the following:

1. If a party wishes the arbitrator to put the witnesses under oath or sequester them, he should request the arbitrator to do so at the beginning of the hearing.

2. If an opening statement is to be presented, it should be clear, concise, and well organized.

3. Exhibits should be presented during the course of the hearing. They should be shown to the other party first before seeking to introduce them.

4. If opposing counsel offers evidence that you believe should not be in the record, make a proper and timely objection.

5. The parties and counsel should avoid unnecessary friction between themselves at the hearing.

6. Direct examination should be to the point, complete but not repetitive.

7. Cross-examination should be used carefully and only in situations where the advocate is almost certain that the testimony obtained through cross-examination will weaken the case of the opposing party.

8. Neither party should attempt to introduce irrelevant material into the record. It will not strengthen his case, and it may cloud the issue for the arbitrator. It also provides grounds for objection.

9. The closing argument made orally or in writing should compellingly and persuasively present the party's theory of the case. It should be well organized, and no longer than it absolutely needs to be. In writing it, significant evidence contrary to your case should not be ignored. Why you believe it does not impact on the quality of your case should be fully explained, if it can be.

Chapter X
Presenting the Case on Written Briefs

Presentation of an arbitration case only through the use of written briefs should ordinarily be done when the parties can stipulate to all the facts and pertinent documents with reference to the dispute. This means that the parties agree completely on exactly what happened, and their dispute is limited to the application of the provisions of the agreement to the agreed facts.

If the parties can stipulate to all the facts and do decide that they wish to present the case on briefs, they should:

1. Prepare a written stipulation of all facts and documents to which the parties have agreed.

2. Agree upon and execute a submission agreement which includes a statement of the issues to be decided by the arbitrator.

3. Select and appoint an arbitrator for the dispute.

4. Agree between themselves as to the dates on which they will:

   a. exchange opening briefs.

   b. exchange rebuttal or closing briefs.

5. Decide whether or not there shall be a deadline date for the decision of the arbitrator. If there is to be a deadline date, the arbitrator should be notified of it at the time of his appointment and his assent obtained to such a condition.

6. Send to the arbitrator:

   a. a copy of a submission agreement.

   b. a jointly signed copy of stipulated facts. If past practice is relevant to the case, it should be included in the stipulated facts. If there is no agreement on past practice, and it is a relevant fact for determining the submitted issue, then it is doubtful that the case is an appropriate one for submission on briefs. The statement of stipulated facts should include all facts and documents necessary for decision of the issue.

c. copies of all agreed-upon evidence, such as the controlling collective bargaining agreement or agreements, reports on grievance committee proceedings, pertinent correspondence between the parties, and all other documentary evidence.

d. copies of the opening and closing briefs. These should be sent to the arbitrator simultaneously with their exchange between the parties.

In this method of arbitration a submission agreement becomes even more important than that in which the case is presented orally. The submission agreement should include all of the following:

1. The agreement to arbitrate the issue.

2. A clear statement of the issue.

3. Appointment of the arbitrator.

4. Dates for exchange of all briefs.

5. Deadline date for arbitrator's award if the parties have decided that a deadline date is necessary. (See Appendix D, Submission Agreements.)

6. A statement that if the arbitrator finds it necessary to obtain further information or to hear further argument after receiving all briefs he shall have the authority to call a hearing or to submit written questions to both parties.

Item 6 is essential in cases presented on written briefs. Often the parties believe that all facts necessary to the decision have been included in the stipulated statement of facts, but in reviewing the case for decision the arbitrator finds that something is missing. He must have the authority to obtain this additional information. His award must be based on a complete presentation of the case. Relevant information should not be excluded from his consideration simply because the parties failed to include it in their formal briefs.

It is difficult to make suggestions on the writing of briefs that will cover all types of cases. But some general statement concerning the organization of the brief and the material which should be included in it can be made. Opening briefs should include at least the following elements, and these elements should be stated in the order in which they are listed below:

1. A statement of the agreed upon issue.

2. A clear, concise statement of the position of the party.

3. The provisions of the agreement involved in the dispute, and analysis of those provisions in terms of the position of the party.

4. Application of the agreement provision to the agreed facts.

5. Argument based upon the party's analysis of the case. The argument should be directed in such a manner as to support the party's position as stated in Item 2 above. At this point, the party should tie together the provisions of the agreement, the stipulated facts, his analysis, and show how all of them support his position.

The rebuttal or closing briefs should be concerned with replying to the other party's opening brief. It should not repeat what was included in the opening brief, nor should it introduce new evidence into the record. The reply should be an attempt to rebut the other party's analysis of the case and position. Specifically, in the rebuttal brief the party should attempt to refute the other party's application of the agreement to the stipulated facts or the emphasis which the opposing party put on certain of the stipulated facts. In other words, the rebuttal brief gives the replying party an opportunity to destroy or lessen the effectiveness of the opposing party's analysis and argument of the case. The rebuttal brief should be limited to that purpose and should not be used as an opportunity to reargue in an affirmative sense the replying party's own position.

Chapter XI
Role of the Arbitrator

The arbitrator is the key person in the arbitration hearing. He or she conducts the hearing. The arbitrator decides and rules on the admissibility of evidence. The arbitrator makes the final and binding decision on the issues submitted to him or her. Clearly, the advocates should constantly keep the arbitrator in mind during the preparation and presentation of the case. If the advocate wishes to win his or her case, it is the arbitrator who must be persuaded. The counsel's job of persuasion will be made easier if the counsel understands the role of the arbitrator and has some insight into the way the arbitrator arrives at the decision.

Arbitrators will, of course, vary in the way they view their roles. Perhaps, however, some helpful information can be obtained by interviewing one arbitrator, recognizing that his answers will not necessarily apply to all arbitrators:

INTERVIEWER: Well, Mr. Arbitrator, how will you decide the case of Ms. Green? It's going to be pretty hard to try to satisfy both sides on this kind of case.

ARBITRATOR: The function of the arbitrator is not to "satisfy" both sides. If the arbitrator conducts a full and fair hearing and makes a fair decision based on the record, that is all the parties have a right to expect of the arbitrator. It may be that the arbitrator will be a "hero" to one side and a "bum" to the other side. But the party who may believe that the arbitrator did not do a good job need not select him or her again. That right is one of the important characteristics of the arbitration process.

INTERVIEWER: Do you think in this case you could have avoided the necessity of making a decision by acting as mediator? Or do you think that an arbitrator shouldn't act as a mediator?

ARBITRATOR: I suppose if I had to say either yes or no to that question, I would have to say no. After all, the parties have asked for arbitration. If they had wanted mediation they could have asked for that. In this case there was no indication that the parties wanted me to try to mediate the dispute involving Ms. Green.

INTERVIEWER: That's right. It was clear that they wanted your decision. How do you intend to rule? Will Ms. Green go back to work?

ARBITRATOR: I don't intend to write my decision during this interview. And certainly the parties have a right to see it before anyone else. After all, you sat in on all the proceedings with the parties' permission. You should be in a good position to write the decision.

INTERVIEWER: It's true, I heard everything you did, but I've never been an arbitrator. Can you give me some idea of how you go about this business of deciding the case?

ARBITRATOR: Yes. First I will try to clearly understand the issue. In this case that's easy. Then I will study the agreement and the written briefs.

INTERVIEWER: What about the record in the case?

ARBITRATOR: That is the most important job. I will study it intensively. I go through the entire transcript, analyzing it carefully, study the exhibits and briefs.

INTERVIEWER: Exactly what do you do when you analyze it?

ARBITRATOR: Well, I weigh the evidence. For example, the important witnesses in this case are, of course, Red and Ms. Green. I will study their testimony to see where they agree and where they disagree. And where they disagree I have to weigh their testimony to see whose statements I believe. In this case the choice will be crucial.

INTERVIEWER: Yes.

ARBITRATOR: You will remember Red first testified that Ms. Green said, "I can't work here any more today." Then he wasn't too sure of that and testified that she might have said, "I'm leaving the store."

INTERVIEWER: That's not what Ms. Green claimed she said.

ARBITRATOR: Yes. And Red said he later told her she was discharged. But Ms. Green claims he didn't say this. This is contradictory testimony. I can't believe both of them. You can see that I will have to decide which one of them to believe.

INTERVIEWER: And from that you will decide whether she quit or was discharged?

ARBITRATOR: Yes. That's one of the first points I must decide. If she quit, then the union's complaint that she was discharged was incorrect and that will end the case.

INTERVIEWER: Suppose you find that she was discharged?

ARBITRATOR: Then I will have to determine whether there was "just cause" for such action. What was the precise basis for the discharge? In this regard, I must decide whose evidence I will accept as to the posting of the house rules.

INTERVIEWER: Suppose you decide the rules were posted, or that in any case Ms. Green knew, as she admitted, that she is required to put the tapes in the package?

ARBITRATOR: Well, there is first a conflict in the evidence as to the tapes. The Detective Company said she did not put the tape in his package. Ms. Green said she always put her tapes in the packages. This evidence about the tapes must be considered carefully. Remember that the detective had no corroboration. He didn't immediately show the package to anybody else. It boils down to his word against hers. Of course, she might be expected to testify that she followed the rules. On the other hand, there is some suggestion in the record that because the detective was doing so many of these investigations and didn't write his reports until later, he could have been confused.

INTERVIEWER: Assume you believe the Detective Company's testimony, what then?

ARBITRATOR: At that point the evidence would add up as follows:

1. The company rules were posted.

2. Ms. Green saw the rules or knew about the tape rule.

3. She did not put the tape in the Detective Company's package.

That doesn't necessarily prove that she made a practice of not putting the tapes in the packages. The Detective Company's report relates to just one instance.

INTERVIEWER: What then?

ARBITRATOR: Then comes the tough problem. Does the evidence so viewed constitute "just cause" for a discharge? At this point the seriousness of the charges must be considered: the fact that no warnings as to the specific incident were given and the fact that no prior warnings were ever issued on this subject. After all, the punishment involved here is what we refer to in labor-management disputes as "economic capital punishment." Should this incident of breaking the rules justify "capital punishment"? The possibility that discharge for the cause stated was an afterthought, that is, that Red was annoyed at Ms. Green concerning the "window-washing" episode and used the "tape" incident as an excuse to terminate her employment, must be considered. Ms. Green's length of service, with no prior adverse record, could be considered.

INTERVIEWER: Couldn't the company argue that Ms. Green was guilty of insubordination because she refused to follow orders and use that as a basis for discharge?

ARBITRATOR: Possibly. But it didn't. A review of the record will show that the company did not rely on that.

If it had, the union might have argued that under the terms of the agreement Ms. Green was not required to wash windows. That, in any case, she did wash the windows. But this was not in issue. The company did not advance it as a basis for discharge and so I cannot consider it in my decision.

INTERVIEWER: Let's suppose that after reviewing the record you discovered that you need some additional information before you can decide. What do you do in a case like that?

Inadequate record

ARBITRATOR: There's only one thing that can be done. Get the missing information. This may mean calling the parties back for a further hearing, or if the information can be obtained in writing, I might direct written questions to both parties. But it is clear that the arbitrator has the responsibility to get the information needed for his decision.

INTERVIEWER: What if you realize during the hearing that the evidence is inadequate? Can you ask questions?

ARBITRATOR: I not only can, but I should ask questions if the needed information has not been supplied. If questions are asked, the arbitrator should limit his or her questions to both counsel and witnesses for the purpose of getting information. He or she should be very careful that he or she doesn't, by questions or any other conduct, give one party or the other what may turn out to be false hopes as to the decision he or she will finally make. Both parties watch closely for any indications of the arbitrator's reaction to the case.

INTERVIEWER: When you write your decision do you put all of your analysis of the record into it?

ARBITRATOR: No, not as such. It certainly is necessary as to background. But there is no necessity to repeat the whole analysis. I try to write a reasonably concise opinion, setting forth the evidence which constitutes the basis for my decision.

INTERVIEWER: I have heard that arbitrators and even judges observe the principles of the "school of anticipatory jurisprudence." Can you explain that to me?

ARBITRATOR: Yes. That school proceeds on this theory: After a complete and thorough study of the record and issue, the arbitrator makes up his mind as to the conclusion he will reach on the issue. He then goes back over the record and drafts the opinion in accordance with his conclusion, drawing support for it from the record. Whether all arbitrators will admit this is the process followed is not in itself important. But the fact that this general mental process is used by many arbitrators either knowingly or unknowingly simply points up the tremendous importance of preparing and presenting each arbitration case adequately and completely. And in presenting the case the advocates should be certain that they have managed to get everything into the record that the arbitrator will need for his or her decision. After all, the arbitrator isn't playing a game of "eenie, meenie, minie, moe—," awarding one for the union, one for the employer. Nor is he or she seeking to compromise the issue. The arbitrator is deciding a case on the basis of the evidence and arguments introduced into the record by the advocates. It is up to the advocates to make that record complete—and to argue the case in such a way as to persuade the arbitrator that their theory of the case presented is the only sound theory, and should therefore be adopted in his decision.

INTERVIEWER: Does your opinion follow any set form?

ARBITRATOR: There is a functional form that I usually follow. An outline of my decision with appropriate headings would ordinarily include the following:

The Issue

Events Leading to the Arbitration

Position of the Parties

Agreement Provisions

Discussion

Then, under "Discussion" in this case I would have a series of subheadings such as these:

Did Ms. Green Quit?

If I decide that she didn't, the next subheading could be:

What Was the Basis for the Discharge?

Company Rules

Did Ms. Green Violate Company Rules?

Warnings

Summary

Under "Summary," I would set forth my final weighing (consideration) of the record and if I decide this is a discharge case then state whether under all the circumstances of the case there was "just cause" for the discharge. If I hold there was no just cause, then I will add a paragraph dealing with the terms of reinstatement and back pay.

INTERVIEWER: Does that end it?

ARBITRATOR: No, my decision or award is always stated in a separate paragraph or paragraphs labeled "Decision" or "Award."

The arrangement may differ from case to case, of course, but what I've just told you is generally the outline of an "Opinion and Award."

INTERVIEWER: I'm still curious. How are you going to decide this case?

ARBITRATOR: Well, as I said earlier, I believe strongly that the parties have the right to be the first to see my decision. I'll send you a copy after they have received theirs. But you don't need to wait for that. Now that you know the way an arbitrator approaches the problem, and you know as much about the case as I do, write your own "Opinion and Award."

Appendix A
Some Legal Aspects of Arbitration

I. Types of Law

In the United States, there are two types of law:

1. *Written law (statutory law):* The Constitution of the United States and the Constitutions of all the States form the fundamental law of this country. All other law must be within the general policies established by these constitutions.

Enactments, or laws, passed by Congress or the state legislatures are called statutes. Acts of cities and counties are called ordinances.

All of these, the Constitutions, federal and state statutes, and ordinances, comprise our written law.

2. *Unwritten law (common law):* This is law developed by courts. When the court has no written law on which to base the decision in a particular controversy, it decides the case on the basis of custom and general principles of right and wrong. These decisions create precedents or rules, which are applied to similar future controversies. The body of law created in this fashion is spoken of as the common law.

Much of the American common law was derived from precedents established by English courts before the American Revolution. American courts have continued to modify the common law through their decisions.

On any specific subject, both bodies of law, common law and statutory law, must be considered. If there is no written law on the subject, then common law, as applied by the courts of the jurisdiction, controls the situation.

If there is a statute on the subject, then the statute and its court interpretations control the situation to the extent the common law has been changed. However, the statute may not cover all aspects of the subject, or it may apply only in certain specified circumstances. Because of this, it is often necessary to consult both common and statutory law.

Law is a volatile field. The law on a subject may be changed by the act of a legislature or by a court decision. This is happening every minute. A particular subject must be checked for the latest laws and decisions on that subject. The summary of legal aspects of arbitration set forth below is a general summary only and is not intended to be an exhaustive analysis of the law of arbitration in any jurisdiction. Even its general validity is limited to the law as it was at the end of 1985. But it is designed to give some indication of matters in this field covered by law.

II. Private Sector Grievance Arbitration

A. Sources of Controlling Law

1. The Early Common Law

Under the early common law developed by the courts, a party could refuse to carry out an agreement to resolve disputes through arbitration at *any* time before the award was issued.[1] This meant that a court would not force a party to arbitrate a particular dispute even if they had previously signed an agreement to do so.[2] Even if evidence was already heard by an arbitrator, a party could back out before any decision and the courts would not interfere.

Under the early common law, courts of the various states did enforce arbitration awards when both parties willingly participated, but the loser thereafter contested the result. At this stage, the award was treated just like a binding contract, written and signed by the parties. For the most part, courts would refuse to consider whether the arbitrator had made erroneous factual or legal conclusions. The award was enforced unless the arbitrator decided something that the parties had not agreed to submit to arbitration.[3]

2. Federal Law Developments

a) United States Arbitration Act

The Federal Arbitration Act was passed in 1925 and codified in 1947.[4] Under this Act, agreements to arbitrate are specifically enforceable if they arise out of "transaction(s) involving commerce" or maritime matters.[5] These categories have been interpreted very broadly by the courts. However, the Federal Arbitration Act specifically excludes "contracts of employment."[6]

---

[1] Bacon Abridgement, Arb. B., Comyns Dig., Arb. D., 5; *Vinyor's Case* 8 Coke, 82.

[2] *Red Cross Line v. Atlantic Fruit Co.*, 264 U.S. 109, 44 S.Ct. 274, 68 L.Ed. 582 (1924).

[3] *See, e.g., Burchell v. Marsh*, 17 How. 344 (1854).

[4] 9 U.S.C. §§1–14.

[5] *Id.* §2.

[6] *Id.* §1.

Federal courts have disagreed as to whether this phrase applies to *collectively* bargained agreements as well as *individual* employment contracts, thereby *excluding* them from coverage of the Act.[7] This question has not been resolved by the U.S. Supreme Court, but with the interpretation of Section 301[8] (see below) there is no longer any real need to determine whether the Federal Arbitration Act covers labor-management agreements to arbitrate.

b) Section 301 of the Labor-Management Relations Act

Section 301 of the Labor-Management Relations Act gives federal district courts jurisdiction over suits for violation of collective bargaining agreements in industries affecting interstate commerce. In 1957, the U.S. Supreme Court, in the *Lincoln Mills*[9] decision, ruled that this section gives the federal courts power to order enforcement of employer-union agreements to arbitrate disputes. The Court in that decision declared: "It seems, therefore, clear to us that Congress adopted a policy which placed sanctions behind agreements to arbitrate grievance disputes, by implication rejecting the common-law rules . . . against enforcement of executory agreements to arbitrate."

In the *Lincoln Mills* decision, the U.S. Supreme Court directed the federal courts to fashion a body of federal substantive law to apply to these cases brought under Section 301 of the Act. Thereafter, the Court rendered three major decisions on certain aspects of arbitration law to be applied by the federal courts in Section 301 suits. These cases—the *Steelworkers Trilogy*—are important, not only for the points of law determined in them, but also for the Courts statements of general policy and attitude toward labor-management arbitration. Because of their importance to this field, the cases are reproduced in Appendix B. Cases arising under the Railway Labor Act generally follow the same policies.

Their holdings may be very briefly summarized as follows:

Steelworkers v. American Manufacturing Co.:[10] The employer refused to arbitrate a grievance seeking reemployment on behalf of an employee who accepted injury benefits based on a 25 percent permanent partial disability. The governing agreement contained a broad arbitration clause. The Court held that courts are "confined to ascertaining whether

---

[7] *Compare Electronics Corp. of Am. v. Electrical Workers (IUE) Local 272*, 492 F.2d 1255, 85 LRRM 2534 (CA 1, 1974) (Act *applies* to collective bargaining agreements) *and Typographical Union No. 23 (Milwaukee) v. Newspapers, Inc.*, 639 F.2d 386, 106 LRRM 2317 (CA 7, 1981) (only collective bargaining agreements in transportation industries are excluded) *with Furniture Workers v. Colonial Hardwood Flooring Co.*, 168 F.2d 33, 22 LRRM 2102 (CA 4, 1948) (Act does *not* apply to collective bargaining agreements.)

[8] 61 Stat. 156, 29 U.S.C. §185.

[9] *Textile Workers v. Lincoln Mills*, 353 U.S. 448, 40 LRRM 2113 (1957).

[10] 363 U.S. 564, 46 LRRM 2414 (1960).

the party seeking arbitration is making a claim which on its face is governed by the contract." If so, then arbitration must be ordered even if the court thinks the claim is frivolous or baseless.

Steelworkers v. Warrior & Gulf Navigation Co.:[11] The employer refused to arbitrate a grievance about subcontracting because the arbitration clause excluded, "matters which are strictly a function of management." The Court held that, "[a]n order to arbitrate the particular grievance should not be denied unless it may be said with positive assurance that the arbitration clause is not susceptible to an interpretation that covers the asserted dispute." The Court demanded "the most forceful evidence" in order to defeat arbitration and required arbitration in the case before it.

Steelworkers v. Enterprise Wheel & Car Corp.:[12] The employer refused to comply with an award requiring reinstatement and payment of back wages to certain employees after the governing agreement expired. The Court held that "courts have no business overruling [an arbitrator] because their interpretation of the contract is different from his." It enforced the award, with a modification requiring that the exact amounts of back pay be arbitrated. The Court's decision stated that enforcement should be denied if an award does not draw "its essence from the collective bargaining agreement."

The major decisions of federal courts *after* the *Steelworkers Trilogy* are summarized in Parts B and C, below.

3. State Law Developments

All states except Oklahoma now have statutes that change or add to the early common law regarding arbitration. Only one of those states (Missouri) has passed a law expressly stating that parties may back out of agreements to arbitrate and file a lawsuit instead.[13] All other state statutes provide more support for arbitration than existed under the early common law. Some state courts, however, have construed statutes narrowly and refused to enforce contracts that provide for arbitration of *any* future dispute under the contract.[14]

Some state statutes expressly *include* collective bargaining agreements.[15] Others make no reference to collective bargaining agreements,[16] or expressly

---

[11] 363 U.S. 574, 46 LRRM 2416 (1960).

[12] 363 U.S. 593, 46 LRRM 2423 (1960).

[13] Mo. Revised Statutes §435.010.

[14] *See, e.g., Kinney v. Baltimore & Ohio Relief Ass'n*, 35 W. Va. 385, 14 S.E. 8 (W. Va. 1891).

[15] California, Colorado, District of Columbia, Indiana, Maine, Massachusetts, Michigan, Minnesota, Nevada, New Jersey, New Mexico, New York, North Carolina, Pennsylvania, Rhode Island, South Dakota, Washington, Wisconsin, and Wyoming.

[16] Arkansas, Connecticut, Florida, Idaho, Illinois, Kansas, Montana, Nebraska, North Dakota, Ohio, Tennessee, Utah, Virginia, and West Virginia.

exclude them.[17] Whatever the state statute says, however, it is clear that state courts which hear cases covered by Section 301 are required to follow federal decisions that develop national labor policy under *Lincoln Mills*.[18]

Nonetheless, state statutes are important for three reasons. First, cases arising under Section 301 may be filed in either federal or state court, and if they are filed in state court, state procedural rules will be followed. Secondly, upon developing federal labor policy under *Lincoln Mills*, federal courts have "borrowed" extensively from state law. For example, a federal court hearing a Section 301 case may decide, as a matter of federal law, to apply the state's time limit for filing and pursuing a case.[19] Lastly, state statutes control many labor agreements that are not subject to Section 301, such as agreements covering local government employees or agricultural workers.

B. The Role Now Played by the Courts *Before* an Arbitration Takes Place

Since *Lincoln Mills* and the *Steelworkers Trilogy*, federal courts have developed the following rules under Section 301 regarding the role to be played by the courts before an arbitration has happened:

1. If one party contends that a particular type of claim is excluded completely from the arbitration clause (as happened in *Warrior Navigation*), arbitration will be compelled if the dispute is *arguably* subject to the arbitration clause. This is called an issue of "substantive" arbitrability.

2. The party who is forced to arbitrate in the above circumstance can then argue to the arbitrator that its actions are free from challenge under the arbitration clause. The arbitrator may then hear and decide two questions: (a) whether the conduct is free from any challenge (the issue of "substantive" arbitrability), and, if *not*, (b) whether the challenge (grievance) should be upheld.[20]

3. If the parties both wish to, they may submit a question of "substantive" arbitrability directly to an arbitrator without asking for a threshold court

---

[17] Alaska, Arizona, Delaware, Iowa, Kentucky, Louisiana, Maryland, New Hampshire, Oregon, and South Carolina.

[18] *Charles Dowd Box Co. v. Courtney*, 368 U.S. 502, 49 LRRM 2619 (1962).

[19] *Auto Workers v. Hoosier Cardinal Corp.*, 383 U.S. 696, 61 LRRM 2545 (1966); *Carpenters Local 1020 v. FMC Corp.*, 724 F.2d 815, 115 LRRM 2582 (CA 9, 1984) (applying Oregon's 20-day limit for actions to vacate arbitration awards).

[20] It should be noted that the Supreme Court's decision in *Warrior Navigation* did not make clear whether the party resisting arbitration may raise an issue about the scope of the arbitration clause in the arbitration hearing itself, *after* having lost the issue before the courts. The lower federal courts, however, have permitted a second "bite at the apple." *See, e.g., Communications Workers v. Western Elec.*, 751 F.2d 203, 118 LRRM 2121 (CA 7, 1984). They have reasoned that since *Warrior Navigation* instructs courts *not* to draw any inferences from bargaining history or practices when hearing petitions to compel arbitration, the party resisting should have an opportunity to present this sort of evidence to the arbitrator. The Supreme Court has not approved or disapproved this application of *Warrior Navigation. See Nolde Bros., Inc. v. Bakery Workers Local 358*, 430 U.S. 243, 255 n.8, 94 LRRM 2753, 2757 (1977).

determination that the claim is *arguably* subject to arbitration. If this is done, the parties are bound by the arbitrator's jurisdictional determination.[21]

4. If one party contends that the other did not follow procedures that are required before arbitration (i.e., time limits or prior steps of the grievance procedure), the court will compel arbitration and leave the question about procedure for the arbitrator to decide.[22] This is called an issue of "procedural" arbitrability.

5. A lawsuit over a claim that is subject to arbitration will be stayed until the arbitration is complete.[23]

6. Even if a dispute arises *after* expiration of a collective bargaining agreement, the courts will require arbitration if the dispute is about the contract's terms and subject to an arbitration clause.[24]

7. If the parties cannot agree upon an arbitrator or a method for selecting one, the court will appoint one upon application of either party.[25] In such a case, suggestions will usually be sought from both parties.

C. The Role Now Played by the Courts *After* an Arbitration Takes Place

A court may be asked to review an award after it is rendered in any of three ways: (1) The prevailing party may ask for court *enforcement* because the loser is not complying; (2) the loser may ask that the award be *vacated*, so that compliance is not required; or (3) either party may ask that the award be *modified*. In each of these cases, the court may grant the relief requested, deny any relief, or *remand* (send back) the case to the arbitrator for further proceedings.

1. Enforcement of the Award

Since *Enterprise Wheel & Car Corp.*, it has been clear that a court requested to enforce an award should *not* review the result in the same way that an appellate court reviews the decision of a trial court. As the U.S. Supreme Court stated in that decision, "The *refusal* of courts to review the *merits* of an arbitration award is the proper approach to arbitration under collective bargaining agreements."[26]

---

[21] *George Day Constr. Co. v. Carpenters Local 354*, 722 F.2d 1471, 115 LRRM 2459 (CA 9, 1984).

[22] *John Wiley & Sons v. Livingston*, 376 U.S. 543, 55 LRRM 2769 (1964).

[23] *Drake Bakeries, Inc. v. Bakery Workers Local 50*, 370 U.S. 254, 50 LRRM 2440 (1962).

[24] *Nolde Bros. v. Bakery Workers Local 358*, 430 U.S. 243, 94 LRRM 2753 (1977).

[25] *Deaton Truck Line, Inc. v. Teamsters Local 612*, 307 F.2d 748, 51 LRRM 2552 (CA 5, 1962).

[26] *Steelworkers v. Enterprise Wheel & Car Corp.*, 363 U.S. 593, 596, 46 LRRM 2423, 2425 (1960).

Thus, a court must enforce an award including the arbitrator's remedy unless the responding party establishes grounds to vacate it (See Section 2 below) *and* the time to seek vacatur has *not* expired. A federal court will refuse to consider *any* objections to an award if the losing party does not raise them within the time allowed for seeking to vacate the award, which is generally very short.[27]

2. *Vacatur of the Award*

Under *Enterprise Wheel & Car Corp.*, "[a] mere ambiguity in the opinion accompanying an award, which permits the inference that the arbitrator may have exceeded his authority, is not a reason for refusing to enforce the award."[28] In keeping with this standard, a small percentage of requests to vacate awards succeed.[29] Lower federal courts have found that an award conclusively exceeds the arbitrator's authority in two primary circumstances:

a) The Award Is Contrary to the Agreement

Although the courts must defer to the arbitrator's construction of the Agreement in any questionable case, some awards have been vacated on the ground that they were contrary to an express and "unambiguous" provision in the Agreement. For example, where the Agreement stated, "false statements made to obtain [sick leave] benefits . . . , will be cause for discharge," and the arbitrator directed reinstatement *after* concluding the grievant provided false statements as described, the award was vacated.[30]

b) The Award Exceeds the Scope of the Submitted Issue

The early common law rule that an award may be vacated if it decides matters the parties did not submit has been preserved as part of the *Enterprise Wheel* test.[31] An arbitrator has no authority apart from that given through agreement of the parties.

---

[27] *Fortune, Alsweet & Eldridge, Inc. v. Daniel Constr Co.*, 724 F.2d 1355, 115 LRRM 2411 (CA 9, 1983) (no defenses to enforcement action considered because losing party did not seek to vacate within 100 days allowed under California statute "borrowed" by federal court). See *supra* note 19 and accompanying text. By contrast, California allows four years to seek enforcement of an award. Cal. Code of Civ. Proc. §1288.

[28] *Steelworkers v. Enterprise Wheel & Car Corp.*, 363 U.S. 593, 598, 46 LRRM 2423, 2425 (1960).

[29] Elkouri & Elkouri, *How Arbitration Works*, 4th ed. (BNA Books, 1985) at 29, note 21, and accompanying text.

[30] *Operating Eng'rs Local 670 v. Kerr-McGee Ref. Corp.*, 618 F.2d 657, 103 LRRM 2988 (CA 10, 1980). *See also Mistletoe Express Serv. v. Motor Expressmen's Union*, 566 F.2d 692, 96 LRRM 3320 (CA 10, 1977); *Teamsters Local 784 v. Ulry-Talbert Co.*, 330 F.2d 562, 55 LRRM 2979 (CA 8, 1964).

[31] *Textile Workers Local 1386 v. American Thread Co.*, 291 F.2d 894, 896, 48 LRRM 2534, 2537 (CA 4, 1961).

Where the submission itself is ambiguous, however, courts must defer to the arbitrator's construction of the submission.[32] For example, an award was upheld in deference to an arbitrator who concluded that postdischarge evidence about a grievant's mental condition at the time misconduct was committed should be considered upon deciding whether the company had "cause" to act at the time of the discharge.[33]

c) Other *Noncontroversial* Grounds

Borrowing from the Federal Arbitration Act and analogous state statutes, courts have stated without controversy that labor arbitration awards may be vacated on two additional grounds: (1) The arbitrator was biased or corrupt;[34] (2) The arbitrator committed misconduct by refusing a postponement despite good cause or by refusing to hear important evidence.[35] It is not frequent that grounds to vacate for either of these reasons exist.[36]

d) Other *Controversial* Grounds

The principles stated thus far regarding vacatur are generally accepted, although different courts may have different views about their correct application in any factual circumstance. Awards have also been vacated on additional grounds that are not uniformly accepted as proper applications of the *Enterprise Wheel* test:

- *Critical Error of Fact*: An award directing reinstatement on the ground that a suspension should have preceded the termination was vacated after the court concluded that a suspension was in fact served before termination.[37] Later decisions emphasize that in this case the court's record made clear that an *erroneous* conclusion of fact was *critical* to the decision.[38] They have refused to apply this precedent where the erroneous *and* critical nature of the fact are not apparent.

- *Contrary to Law or "Public Policy"*: The courts are in total disagreement regarding the extent to which courts should reconsider legal issues resolved by arbitrators. Some decisions say that a party who submits a

---

[32] *W.R. Grace & Co. v. Rubber Workers Local 759*, 461 U.S. 757, 765, 113 LRRM 2641, 2644 (1983).

[33] *Mobil Oil Corp. v. Oil Workers Local 8-831*, 679 F.2d 299, 110 LRRM 2620 (CA 3, 1982).

[34] 9 U.S.C. §10(b).

[35] 9 U.S.C. §10(c).

[36] *See, e.g., Builders Supply Co. v. Teamsters Local 123*, 703 F.2d 324, 112 LRRM 3300 (CA 8, 1983); *Grahams Serv., Inc. v. Teamsters Local 975*, 700 F.2d 420, 111 LRRM 2916 (CA 8, 1982).

[37] *Electronics Corp. of Am. v. Electrical Workers (IUE) Local 272*, 492 F.2d 1255, 85 LRRM 2534 (CA 1, 1974). *See also Storer Broadcasting Co. v. Television & Radio Artists*, 600 F.2d 45, 101 LRRM 2497 (CA 6, 1979).

[38] See *Ford Parcel Serv., Inc. v. Teamsters Local 610*, 656 F.2d 387, 108 LRRM 2227 (CA 8, 1981).

legal question to arbitration is bound by the decision.[39] Others say it may be reviewed and vacated if it displays a "manifest disregard" for the law or requires an illegal act.[40] Still others take a middle approach and state that a court should review whether the arbitrator used the correct legal "standard," but should not review how it was applied to the facts.[41] The U.S. Supreme Court has not spoken definitively on this topic but it has given some guidance.

In *W.R. Grace & Co. v. Rubber Workers Local 759*,[42] an award was challenged on the ground that it was inconsistent with an EEOC conciliation agreement. The U.S. Supreme Court upheld the award, but commented enforcement of awards may be denied if they violate some "explicit public policy." The Court further said,

"Such a public policy, however, must be well defined and dominant, and is to be ascertained 'by reference to the laws and legal precedents and not from general considerations of supposed public interests.' [citation omitted]"[43]

- *Contrary to Prior Award*: More than one decision has vacated an award on the ground that it was contrary to the "common law" of the industry as expressed in prior arbitral decisions.[44] This is inconsistent with a U.S. Supreme Court decision requiring courts to defer to an arbitrator's conclusions about his or her authority to overturn prior arbitration awards.[45]

3. Modification of the Award

The Federal Arbitration Act provides for judicial modification of awards if: (1) there is an evident miscalculation, (2) an imperfection of form, or (3) a decision on a matter *not* submitted that can be excised without affecting decisions on things that *were* submitted.[46] None of these circumstances are frequent in labor arbitration.

---

[39] *Jones Dairy Farm v. Food & Commercial Workers Local P-1236*, 760 F.2d 173, 119 LRRM 2185 (CA 7, 1985).

[40] *Postal Workers v. United States Postal Serv.*, 682 F.2d 1280, 110 LRRM 2764 (CA 9, 1982).

[41] *Broadway Cab Coop., Inc. v. Teamsters Local 281*, 710 F.2d 1379, 113 LRRM 3561 (CA 9, 1983).

[42] 461 U.S. 757, 113 LRRM 2641 (1983).

[43] *Id.* at 766, 113 LRRM at 2645.

[44] *Clinchfield Coal Co. v. Mine Workers Dist. 28*, 736 F.2d 998, 116 LRRM 2884 (CA 4, 1984); *Clinchfield Coal Co. v. Mine Workers Dist. 28*, 720 F.2d 1365, 114 LRRM 3053 (CA 4, 1983).

[45] *See supra* note 32 and accompanying text.

[46] 9 U.S.C. §11.

4. Remand for Arbitration

The traditional rule is that, "once an arbitrator has made and published a final award his authority is exhausted and he is *functus officio* and can do nothing more in regard to the subject matter of the arbitration."[47] This policy assures that no party has a reason to put pressure on an arbitrator that might result in reversal of a decision. Since the arbitrator has no authority to reconsider, there is no incentive for pressure or enticements. It also assures that prolonged efforts to secure reconsideration will not prevent the award from promptly ending the dispute in a final and binding way.

The courts have carved out several exceptions to this rule in circumstances where the danger motivating it is not present:

- There is a mistake warranting correction which is obvious on the face of the award.[48]

- The award is incomplete, leaving part of the submitted issue(s) unresolved.[49]

- There is a dispute as to whether the loser has properly complied with the award.[50]

- Changed facts suggest that the arbitrator's original *remedy* may be futile or inappropriate.[51]

None of these exceptions allow the arbitrator to change a decision on the merits. They instead invite attention to topics not yet addressed by the arbitrator.[52]

When one party seeks enforcement, vacatur, or modification, the court may conclude that further arbitration proceedings are warranted under one of these exceptions and remand the case.

D. Two Bites at the Apple?

Ordinarily, an agreement's grievance and arbitration procedure is the *exclusive* channel for resolving claims that arise out of the agreement, includ-

---

[47] *La Vale Plaza, Inc. v. R.S. Noonan, Inc.*, 378 F.2d 569, 572 (CA 3, 1967).

[48] *Id.* at 573.

[49] *See supra* note 12 and accompanying text.

[50] *Hanford Atomic Metal Trades Council v. General Elec. Co.*, 353 F.2d 302, 61 LRRM 2004 (CA 9, 1965).

[51] *Teamsters Local 115 v. DeSoto, Inc.*, 725 F.2d 931, 115 LRRM 2449 (CA 3, 1984).

[52] Some decisions have remanded cases to the arbitrator seeking clarification because one possible construction of the award would make it subject to vacatur. See *Textron, Inc. v. Machinists Lodge 1076*, 648 F.2d 462, 107 LRRM 2836 (CA 7, 1981). This does not comply with *Enterprise Wheel's* instruction that "mere ambiguities" should not stand in the way of enforcement. See *supra* note 28 and accompanying text.

ing discharge. An employee may not ignore that procedure and file a lawsuit over contract rights.[53] There are three major circumstances, however, in which arbitration may not end dispute over an employee's complaints.

1. Title VII and Other Claims Based on Statutes or Public Policy

In a case involving claims of race discrimination, *Alexander v. Gardner-Denver Co.*,[54] the U.S. Supreme Court held that even though an arbitration award found termination was for "just cause," the federal courts should give the case a fresh look. The Court stated, "The federal court should consider the employee's claim *de novo*."[55] In a now famous footnote, the Court explained that in future cases it might be appropriate for the Court to put some reliance on a prior arbitration award:

> "We adopt no standards as to the weight to be accorded an arbitral decision, since this must be determined in the court's discretion with regard to the facts and circumstances of each case. Relevant factors include the existence of provisions in the collective-bargaining agreement that conform substantially with Title VII, the degree of procedural fairness in the arbitral forum, *adequacy of the record* with respect to the issue of discrimination, and the special competence of particular arbitrators. *Where an arbitral determination gives full consideration to an employee's Title VII rights, a court may properly accord it great weight.* This is especially true where the issue is solely one of fact, specifically addressed by the parties and decided by the arbitrator on the basis of an adequate record. But courts should ever be mindful that Congress, in enacting Title VII, thought it necessary to provide a judicial forum for the ultimate resolution of discriminatory employment claims. It is the duty of courts to assure the full availability of this forum." (emphasis added)[56]

There is every reason to believe that the same policy applies in the case of other claims that might be raised under Title VII, such as claims of sexual harassment or religious discrimination.[57] This is of importance because sexual harassment is an increasingly frequent issue in arbitration. It generally comes up in one of two ways.

A discharged employee may claim that he or she was the victim of sexual harassment. Here, *Gardner-Denver*[58] applies. Thus, if either party hopes to

---

[53] *Republic Steel Corp. v. Maddox*, 379 U.S. 650, 58 LRRM 2193 (1965).

[54] 415 U.S. 36, 7 FEP Cases 81 (1974).

[55] *Id.* at 60, 7 FEP Cases at 90.

[56] *Id.*

[57] *Kremer v. Chemical Constr. Corp.*, 456 U.S. 461, 28 FEP Cases 1412, 1419 (1982) (referring to *Gardner-Denver* as controlling no matter what kind of employment discrimination is alleged). See also *Rabidue v. Osceola Ref. Co.*, 584 F.Supp. 419, 36 FEP 183 (ED Mich, 1984); *Cummings v. Walsh Constr. Co.*, 561 F.Supp. 872, 31 FEP Cases 930 (SD Ga, 1983).

[58] *Supra* note 54.

rely upon the award in the event of Title VII litigation, that party should make certain there is a complete record (transcript) of the arbitration and that the harassment issue is fully presented and considered.

The issue also arises in cases where the employer terminates an employee believed to have been *responsible* for sexual harassment of co-workers. In one reported case, a male employee discharged for that reason lost in arbitration and later sued the accusing female witnesses for defamation and injury to his reputation. The court found the arbitrator's finding that the accusations of harassment were truthful barred this lawsuit.[59]

The reasoning of *Gardner-Denver* has been applied by the courts to find that civil lawsuits may proceed after arbitration under other civil rights statutes,[60] under the Fair Labor Standards Act,[61] which controls minimum wages and overtime rates, and under the Employee Retirement Income Security Act,[62] which controls retirement and pension benefits.

Separate lawsuits have also been allowed after arbitration where a discharge has assertedly violated an important public policy of the state.[63] In this circumstance, a court may be unwilling to accept a private arbitrator as an adequate guardian of the public interest.

2. Claims of Anti-Union Discrimination

If an employee grieves, claiming discrimination by the employer because of union activity, a charge that the employer has committed an unfair labor practice ("ULP") in violation of the National Labor Relations Act[64] may also be filed. There are other circumstances in which both a ULP charge and a grievance may turn on the same facts.

The National Labor Relations Board, which administers the NLRA, has followed various policies over the years as to when it will require a complaining employee to arbitrate and when it will accept an arbitrator's findings as binding.

At present, the Board will require a discharged employee under a collective bargaining agreement to arbitrate any claim of anti-union discrimination.[65] If the case already has been arbitrated when it comes to the Board's attention, the Board will accept the award as binding if: (1) the contract and ULP issues

---

[59] Barnes v. Oody, 514 F.Supp. 23, 28 FEP Cases 816 (ED Tenn, 1981).

[60] McDonald v. City of West Branch, Mich., 466 U.S. 284, 115 LRRM 3646 (1984); Bectan v. Detroit Terminal, 687 F.2d 140, 29 FEP Cases 1078 (CA 6, 1982).

[61] Barrentine v. Arkansas-Best Freight Sys., 450 U.S. 728, 24 WH Cases 1284 (1981).

[62] Amaro v. Continental Can Co., 724 F.2d 747, 5 EBC 1215 (CA 9, 1984).

[63] Garibaldi v. Lucky Food Stores, 726 F.2d 1367, 115 LRRM 3089 (CA 9, 1984).

[64] 29 U.S.C. §1 et seq.

[65] United Technologies Corp., 268 NLRB 557, 115 LRRM 1049 (1984).

are *factually parallel*, (2) the facts relevant to the ULP issue were *generally presented* to the arbitrator, (3) the proceedings were *fair*, and (4) the result is *not repugnant* to the purposes and policies of the NLRA.[66] These last two requirements are applied by the Board in all cases where one side asserts an award should be accepted as conclusive.[67]

3. Employee Claims Under Section 301

The U.S. Supreme Court has held that a union owes a duty to fairly represent every member of the bargaining unit.[68] In *Hines v. Anchor Motor Freight, Inc.*,[69] the Court held that an employee may bring a suit under Section 301 claiming that union presentation of a grievance at arbitration did not comply with the duty of fair representation. The Court further held that where bad-faith performance of the union is established,[70] the employee should be allowed to present the merits of the grievance against the employer in court. This means that both parties to an arbitration have a strong incentive to assure that the grievant receives a full and fair hearing.

III. Public Sector Grievance Arbitration[71]

A. Federal Employees

Collective bargaining and grievance arbitration for federal employees are controlled by the Civil Service Reform Act of 1978.[72] Under the CSRA, collective agreements *must* provide a grievance and arbitration procedure applicable to all complaints except those specifically excluded by the agreement or statute.[73] Policies followed by courts when one party seeks to compel arbitration are analogous to those spawned by the *Trilogy* in the private sector

---

[66] *Olin Corp.*, 268 NLRB 573, 115 LRRM 1056 (1984).

[67] *Spielberg Mfg. Co.*, 112 NLRB 1080, 36 LRRM 1152 (1955).

[68] *Vaca v. Sipes*, 386 U.S. 171, 64 LRRM 2369 (1967).

[69] 424 U.S. 554, 91 LRRM 2481 (1976).

[70] Lower courts disagree as to whether a complaining employee must show willful bad faith, or whether negligent conduct can breach the duty. *Compare Dutrisac v. Caterpillar Tractor Co.*, 749 F.2d 1270, 113 LRRM 3532 (CA 9, 1983) (negligent failure to pursue a grievance breached the duty) *with Ruzicka v. General Motors Corp.*, 649 F.2d 1207, 107 LRRM 2726 (CA 6, 1981) (simple negligence insufficient).

[71] What is provided here briefly highlights critical legal distinctions between private and public sector grievance arbitration. For a fuller summary, see Elkouri & Elkouri, *How Arbitration Works*, 4th ed. (BNA Books, 1985) 46–95.

[72] 5 U.S.C. §1101 *et seq.*

[73] Under the CSRA, individual employees who are complaining about specified adverse actions or discrimination may choose between the grievance/arbitration procedure and alternate statutory remedies.

with one exception. The conclusion that a particular topic is under management's unbridled control and *not* subject to grievance is far more frequent. This is so because statutes and regulations that have no application to private employers preserve the government's right to manage in many areas.

The role of arbitrators under federal collective agreements differs in a significant respect from the private sector.[74] That difference directly affects the extent to which awards are reviewable. Since under the CSRA *all* complaints are subject to arbitration (unless excepted), arbitrators interpret not only the agreement, but also controlling statutes, rules, and regulations. Congress did not contemplate giving arbitrators a final say on these matters, as would result from application of *Trilogy* principles. Rather, more clearly defined systems for review exist.

Any party may seek review by the Federal Labor Relations Authority, unless the grievance involves specified adverse action against an employee, such as reduction in grade or removal for poor performance.[75] These cases are subject to a different review system. The FLRA may find the award deficient: "1) because it is contrary to any law, rule or regulation; or 2) on other grounds similar to those applied by Federal courts in private sector labor-management relations."[76] The FLRA's decision is final unless an unfair labor practice issue is involved.

Cases involving specified adverse action against individual employees may be taken directly to a federal court of appeals. If management is complaining about the result, the grounds for review are just as limited as in the private sector.[77] The CSRA, however, creates additional grounds for review if the aggrieved employee attacks the award. Section 7703(c) then requires the court to set aside any findings or conclusions found to be:

"(1) arbitrary, capricious, an abuse of discretion, or otherwise not in accordance with law;

"(2) obtained without procedures required by law, rule, or regulation having been followed; or

"(3) unsupported by substantial evidence."

This addition was made to assure uniformity in the protection of government employee's rights.

---

[74] See Kagel, "Grievance Arbitration in the Federal Service: Still Hardly Final and Binding," in J.L. Stern & B.D. Dennis, eds., *Arbitration Issues for the 1980s, Proceedings of the 34th Annual Meeting, National Academy of Arbitrators* (BNA Books, 1982) at 178.

[75] 5 U.S.C. §§4303, 7121, 7122, and 7512.

[76] 5 U.S.C. §7122(a).

[77] *Devine v. White,* 697 F.2d 421, 439, 112 LRRM 2374, 2387 (CA DC, 1983).

B. State and Local Government Employees

Few generalities can be stated regarding the treatment of grievance arbitration for state and local government employees in the various states.[78] Policies vary widely, and in each instance one must consult the state's Constitution and statutes, local charters and ordinances, *and* court decisions. In the majority of states it is lawful for at least certain categories of public employees to organize and secure arbitration agreements. Many private sector principles are followed in analogous circumstances, but there are noteworthy exceptions.

For example, in contrast to the *Trilogy* rule that all arguable cases should go to arbitration, New York requires an "express, direct and unequivocal" arbitration commitment under its Taylor Law.[79]

As in the case of federal employment, issues far more frequently arise as to whether a particular topic is, by law, within management's unbridled discretion or otherwise nonarbitrable. For example, a California decision holds that certain employees may not enter into agreements calling for arbitration of discharge cases because a statutory procedure exists to review such decisions.[80] This decision was met by proposals for statutory reform.[81] Changes regarding specific issues that arise in public sector grievance arbitration are frequent and thorough; current research of any question is required.

---

[78] See generally, Craver, "The Judicial Enforcement of Public Sector Grievance Arbitration," 58 *Tex. L. Rev.* 329 (1980).

[79] *Acting Superintendent of Liverpool Cent. School Dist. v. United Liverpool Faculty Ass'n,* 369 N.E.2d 746, 747, 96 LRRM 2779 (N.Y. Ct. App., 1977).

[80] *Steelworkers Local 8599 v. Fontana Unified School Dist.,* 162 Cal. App.3d 823, 209 Cal. Rptr. 16 (4th Dist., 1984).

[81] 4:2 *Lab. & Empl. L. News* (Fall, 1985) at 1.

Appendix B

The Steelworkers Trilogy

United Steelworkers of America v. American Manufacturing Company

Supreme Court of the United States
363 U.S. 564, 46 LRRM 2414 (1960)

Full Text of Opinion

MR. JUSTICE DOUGLAS delivered the opinion of the Court.

This suit was brought by petitioner union in the District Court to compel arbitration of a "grievance" that petitioner, acting for one Sparks, a union member, had filed with the respondent, Sparks' employer. The employer defended on the ground (1) that Sparks is estopped from making his claim because he had a few days previously settled a workmen's compensation claim against the company on the basis that he was permanently partially disabled, (2) that Sparks is not physically able to do the work, and (3) that this type of dispute is not arbitrable under the collective bargaining agreement in question.

[PROVISIONS OF CONTRACT]

The agreement provided that during its term there would be "no strike," unless the employer refused to abide by a decision of the arbitrator. The agreement sets out a detailed grievance procedure with a provision for arbitration (regarded as the standard form) of all disputes between the parties

146

"as to the meaning, interpretation and application of the provisions of this agreement."[1]

The agreement also reserves to the management power to suspend or discharge any employee "for cause."[2] It also contains a provision that the employer will employ and promote employees on the principle of seniority "where ability and efficiency are equal."[3] Sparks left his work due to an injury and while off work brought an action for compensation benefits. The case was settled, Sparks' physician expressing the opinion that the injury had made him 25% permanently partially disabled. That was on September 9. Two weeks later the union filed a grievance which charged that Sparks was entitled to return to his job by virtue of the seniority provision of the collective bargaining agreement. Respondent refused to arbitrate and this action was brought. The District Court held that Sparks, having accepted the settlement on the basis of permanent partial disability was estopped to claim any seniority or employment rights and granted the motion for summary judgment. The Court of Appeals affirmed, 264 F. 2d 624, 43 LRRM 2757, for different reasons. After reviewing the evidence it held that the grievance is "a frivolous, patently baseless one, not subject to arbitration under the collective bargaining agreement." Id., at 628. The case is here on a writ of certiorari, 361 U.S. 881.

[POLICY OF LMRA]

Section 203(d) of the Labor Management Relations Act, 1947, 61 Stat. 154, 29 U.S.C. § 173(d) states, "Final adjustment by a method agreed upon by the parties is hereby declared to be the desirable method for settlement of grievance disputes arising over the application or interpretation of an existing

---

[1]The relevant arbitration provisions read as follows:

"Any disputes, misunderstandings, differences or grievances arising between the parties as to the meaning, interpretation and application of the provisions of this agreement, which are not adjusted as herein provided, may be submitted to the Board of Arbitration for decision. . . ."

"The arbitrator may interpret this agreement and apply it to the particular case under consideration but shall, however, have no authority to add to, subtract from, or modify the terms of the agreement. Disputes relating to discharges or such matters as might involve a loss of pay for employees may carry an award of back pay in whole or in part as may be determined by the Board of Arbitration.

"The decision of the Board of Arbitration shall be final and conclusively binding upon both parties, and the parties agree to observe and abide by same. . . ."

[2]"The Management of the works, the direction of the working force, plant layout and routine of work, including the right to hire, suspend, transfer, discharge or otherwise discipline any employee for cause, such cause being: infraction of company rules, inefficiency, insubordination, contagious disease harmful to others, and any other ground or reason that would tend to reduce or impair the efficiency of plant operation; and to lay off employees because of lack of work, is reserved to the Company, provided it does not conflict with this agreement. . . ."

[3]This provision provides in relevant part:

"The Company and the Union fully recognize the principle of seniority as a factor in the selection of employees for promotion, transfer, lay-off, re-employment, and filling of vacancies, where ability and efficiency are equal. It is the policy of the Company to promote employees on that basis."

collective-bargaining agreement. . . ." That policy can be effectuated only if the means chosen by the parties for settlement of their differences under a collective bargaining agreement is given full play.

A state decision that held to the contrary announced a principle that could only have a crippling effect on grievance arbitration. The case was *International Assn. of Machinists v. Cutler-Hammer, Inc.*, 271 App. Div. 917, 19 LRRM 2232, aff'd, 297 N.Y. 519, 20 LRRM 2445. It held that "If the meaning of the provision of the contract sought to be arbitrated is beyond dispute, there cannot be anything to arbitrate and the contract cannot be said to provide for arbitration." 271 App. Div., at 918. The lower courts in the instant case had a like preoccupation with ordinary contract law. The collective agreement requires arbitration of claims that courts might be unwilling to entertain. Yet in the context of the plant or industry the grievance may assume proportions of which judges are ignorant. Moreover, the agreement is to submit all grievances to arbitration, not merely those that a court may deem to be meritorious. There is no exception in the "no strike" clause and none therefore should be read into the grievance clause, since one is the *quid pro quo* for the other.[4] The question is not whether in the mind of a court there is equity in the claim. Arbitration is a stabilizing influence only as it serves as a vehicle for handling every and all disputes that arise under the agreement.

[FUNCTION OF COURT]

The collective agreement calls for the submission of grievances in the categories which it describes irrespective of whether a court may deem them to be meritorious. In our role of developing a meaningful body of law to govern the interpretation and enforcement of collective bargaining agreements, we think special need should be given to the context in which collective bargaining agreements are negotiated and the purpose which they are intended to serve. See *Lewis v. Benedict Coal Corp.*, 361 U.S. 459, 468, 45 LRRM 2719. The function of the court is very limited when the parties have agreed to submit all questions of contract interpretation to the arbitrator. It is then confined to ascertaining whether the party seeking arbitration is making a claim which on its face is governed by the contract. Whether the moving party is right or wrong is a question of contract interpretation for the arbitrator. In these circumstances the moving party should not be deprived of the arbitrator's judgment, when it was his judgment and all that it connotes that was bargained for.

The courts therefore have no business weighing the merits of the grievance,[5] considering whether there is equity in a particular claim, or

---

[4]Cf. *Structural Steel & Ornament Assn. v. Shopmen's Local Union*, 172 F. Supp. 354, 43 LRRM 2868, where the company sued for breach of the "no strike" agreement.

[5]See *New Bedford Defense Products Division v. Local No. 1113*, 258 F. 2d, 522, 42 LRRM 2518 (C.A. 1st Cir 1958).

determining whether there is particular language in the written instrument which will support the claim. The agreement is to submit all grievances to arbitration, not merely those the court will deem meritorious. The processing of even frivolous claims may have therapeutic values which those who are not a part of the plant environment may be quite unaware.[6]

The union claimed in this case that the company had violated a specific provision of the contract. The company took the position that it had not violated that clause. There was, therefore, a dispute between the parties as to "the meaning, interpretation and application" of the collective bargaining agreement. Arbitration should have been ordered. When the judiciary undertakes to determine the merits of a grievance under the guise of interpreting the grievance procedure of collective bargaining agreements, it usurps a function which under that regime is entrusted to the arbitration tribunal.

Reversed.

MR. JUSTICE FRANKFURTER concurs in the result.

MR. JUSTICE WHITTAKER, believing that the District Court lacked jurisdiction to determine the merits of the claim which the parties had validly agreed to submit to the exclusive jurisdiction of a Board of Arbitrators (*Textile Workers v. Lincoln Mills*, 353 U.S. 448, 40 LRRM 2113, 2120), concurs in the result of this opinion.

MR. JUSTICE BLACK took no part in the consideration or decision of this case.

United Steelworkers of America v. Warrior and Gulf Navigation Company

Supreme Court of the United States
363 U.S. 574, 46 LRRM 2416 (1960)

Full Text of Opinion

MR. JUSTICE DOUGLAS delivered the opinion of the Court.

Respondent transports steel and steel products by barge and maintains a terminal at Chicasaw, Alabama, where it performs maintenance and repair

---

[6]Cox, Current Problems in the Law of Grievance Arbitration, 30 Rocky Mt. L. Rev. 247, 261 (1958), writes:

"The typical arbitration clause is written in words which cover, without limitation, all disputes concerning the interpretation or application of a collective bargaining agreement. Its words do not restrict its scope to meritorious disputes or two-sided disputes, still less are they limited to disputes which a judge will consider two-sided. Frivolous cases are often taken, and are expected to be taken, to arbitration. What one man considers frivolous another may find meritorious, and it is common knowledge in industrial relations circles that grievance arbitration often serves as a safety valve for troublesome complaints. Under these circumstances it seems proper to read the typical arbitration clause as a promise to arbitrate every claim, meritorious or frivolous, which the complainant bases upon the contract. The objection that equity will not order a party to do a useless act is outweighed by the cathartic value of arbitrating even a frivolous grievance and by the dangers of excessive judicial intervention."

work on its barges. The employees at that terminal constitute a bargaining unit covered by a collective bargaining agreement negotiated by petitioner union. Respondent between 1956 and 1958 laid off some employees, reducing the bargaining unit from 42 to 23 men. This reduction was due in part to respondent contracting maintenance work, previously done by its employees, to other companies. The latter used respondent's supervisors to lay out the work and hired some of the laid-off employees of respondent (at reduced wages). Some were in fact assigned to work on respondent's barges. A number of employees signed a grievance which petitioner presented to respondent, the grievance reading:

"We are hereby protesting the Company's actions, of arbitrarily and unreasonably contracting out work to other concerns, that could and previously has been performed by Company employees.

"This practice becomes unreasonable, unjust and discriminatory in view of the fact that at present there are a number of employees that have been laid off for about 1 and ½ years or more for allegedly lack of work.

"Confronted with these facts we charge that the Company is in violation of the contract by inducing a partial lockout, of a number of the employees who would otherwise be working were it not for this unfair practice."

[GRIEVANCE PROCEDURE]

The collective agreement had both a "no strike" and a "no lockout" provision. It also had a grievance procedure which provided in relevant part as follows:

"Issues which conflict with any Federal statute in its application as established by Court procedure or matters which are strictly a function of management shall not be subject to arbitration under this section.

"Should differences arise between the Company and the Union or its members employed by the Company as to the meaning and application of the provisions of this Agreement, or should any local trouble of any kind arise, there shall be no suspension of work on account of such differences but an earnest effort shall be made to settle such differences immediately in the following manner:

"A. For Maintenance Employees:

"First, between the aggrieved employees, and the Foreman involved; Second, between a member or members of the Grievance Committee designated by the Union, and the Foreman and Master Mechanics."

. . .

"Fifth, if agreement has not been reached the matter shall be referred to an impartial umpire for decision. The parties shall meet to decide on an umpire acceptable to both. If no agreement on selection of an umpire is reached the parties shall jointly petition the United States Conciliation Service for suggestion of a list of umpires from which selection will be made. The decision of the umpire shall be final."

Settlement of this grievance was not had and respondent refused arbitration. This suit was then commenced by the union to compel it.[1]

[THEORY OF COURTS BELOW]

The District Court granted respondent's motion to dismiss the complaint. 168 F. Supp. 702, 43 LRRM 2328. It held after hearing evidence, much of which went to the merits of the grievance, that the agreement did not "confide in an arbitrator the right to review the defendant's business judgment in contracting out work." *Id.* at 705. It further held that "the contracting out of repair and maintenance work, as well as construction work, is strictly a function of management not limited in any respect by the labor agreement involved here." *Ibid.* The Court of Appeals affirmed by a divided vote, 269 F. 2d 633, 44 LRRM 2567, the majority holding that the collective agreement had withdrawn from the grievance procedure "matters which are strictly a function of management" and that contracting-out fell in that exception. The case is here on a writ of certiorari, 361 U.S. 912.

We held in *Textile Workers v. Lincoln Mills*, 353 U.S. 448, 40 LRRM 2113, 2120, that a grievance arbitration provision in a collective agreement could be enforced by reason of § 301 (a) of the Labor Management Relations Act[2] and that the policy to be applied in enforcing this type of arbitration was that reflected in our national labor laws. *Id.*, at 456–457. The present federal policy is to promote industrial stabilization through the collective bargaining agreement.[3] *Id.*, at 453–454. A major factor in achieving industrial peace is the inclusion of a provision for arbitration of grievances in the collective bargaining agreement.[4]

---

[1]Section 301 (a) of the Labor Management Relations Act, 1947, 61 Stat. 156, 29 U.S.C. § 185 (a), provides:

"Suits for violation of contracts between an employer and a labor organization representing employees in an industry affecting commerce as defined in this Act, or between any such labor organizations, may be brought in any district court of the United States having jurisdiction of the parties, without respect to the amount in controversy or without regard to the citizenship of the parties." See *Textile Workers v. Lincoln Mills*, 353 U.S. 448.

[2]Note 1, *supra.*

[3]In § 8 (d) of the 1947 Act, 29 U.S.C. § 158 (d), Congress indeed provided that where there was a collective agreement for a fixed term the duty to bargain did not require either party "to discuss or agree to any modification of the terms and conditions contained in" the contract. And see *Labor Board v. Sands Mfg. Co.*, 306 U.S. 332, 4 LRRM 530.

[4]Complete effectuation of the federal policy is achieved when the agreement contains both an arbitration provision for all unresolved grievances and an absolute prohibition of strikes, the arbitration agreement being the *"quid pro quo"* for the agreement not to strike. *Textile Workers v. Lincoln Mills*, 353 U.S. 448, 455.

Thus the run of arbitration cases, illustrated by *Wilko v. Swan*, 346 U.S. 427, become irrelevant to our problem. There the choice is between the adjudication of cases or controversies in courts with established procedures or even special statutory safeguards on the one hand and the settlement of them in the more informal arbitration tribunal on the other. In the commercial case, arbitration is the substitute for litigation. Here arbitration is the substitute for industrial strife. Since arbitration of labor disputes has quite different functions from arbitration under an ordinary commercial agreement, the hostility evinced by courts toward arbitration of commercial agreements has no place here. For arbitration of labor disputes under collective bargaining agreements is part and parcel of the collective bargaining process itself.

[COLLECTIVE AGREEMENT]

The collective bargaining agreement states the rights and duties of the parties. It is more than a contract, it is a generalized code to govern a myriad of cases which the draftsmen cannot wholly anticipate. See Shulman, Reason, Contract, and Law in Labor Relations, 68 Harv. L. Rev. 999, 1004–1005. The collective agreement covers the whole employment relationship.[5] It calls into being a new common law—the common law of a particular industry or of a particular plant. As one observer has put it:[6]

"...[I]t is not unqualifiedly true that a collective-bargaining agreement is simply a document by which the union and employees have imposed upon management limited, express restrictions of its otherwise absolute right to manage the enterprise, so that an employee's claim must fail unless he can point to a specific contract provision upon which the claim is founded. There are too many people, too many problems, too many unforeseeable contingencies to make the words of the contract the exclusive source of rights and duties. One cannot reduce all the rules governing community

---

[5]"Contracts which ban strikes often provide for lifting the ban under certain conditions. Unconditional pledges against strikes are, however, somewhat more frequent than conditional ones. Where conditions are attached to no-strike pledges, one or both of two approaches may be used: certain *subjects* may be exempted from the scope of the pledge, or the pledge may be lifted after certain *procedures* are followed by the union. (Similar qualifications may be made in pledges against lockouts.)

"Most frequent conditions for lifting no-strike pledges are: (1) The occurrence of a deadlock in wage reopening negotiations; and (2) violation of the contract, especially non-compliance with the grievance procedure and failure to abide by an arbitration award.

"No-strike pledges may also be lifted after compliance with specified procedures. Some contracts permit the union to strike after the grievance procedure has been exhausted without a settlement, and where arbitration is not prescribed as the final recourse. Other contracts permit a strike if mediation efforts fail, or after a specified cooling-off period." Collective Bargaining Negotiations and Contracts, Bureau of National Affairs, Inc., 77:101.

[6]Cox, Reflections Upon Labor Arbitration, 72 Harv. L. Rev. 1482, 1498–1499 (1959).

like an industrial plant to fifteen or even fifty pages. Within the sphere of collective bargaining, the institutional characteristics and the governmental nature of the collective-bargaining process demand a common law of the shop which implements and furnishes the context of the agreement. We must assume that intelligent negotiators acknowledged so plain a need unless they stated a contrary rule in plain words."

A collective bargaining agreement is an effort to erect a system of industrial self-government. When most parties enter into contractual relationship they do so voluntarily, in the sense that there is no real compulsion to deal with one another, as opposed to dealing with other parties. This is not true of the labor agreement. The choice is generally not between entering or refusing to enter into a relationship, for that in all probability pre-exists the negotiations. Rather it is between having that relationship governed by an agreed upon rule of law or leaving each and every matter subject to a temporary resolution dependent solely upon the relative strength, at any given moment, of the contending forces. The mature labor agreement may attempt to regulate all aspects of the complicated relationship, from the most crucial to the most minute over an extended period of time. Because of the compulsion to reach agreement and the breadth of the matters covered, as well as the need for a fairly concise and readable instrument, the product of negotiations (the written document) is, in the words of the late Dean Shulman, "a compilation of diverse provisions; some provide objective criteria almost automatically applicable; some provide more or less specific standards which require reason and judgment in their application; and some do little more than leave problems to future consideration with an expression of hope and good faith." Shulman, *supra*, at 1005. Gaps may be left to be filled in by reference to the practices of the particular industry and of the various shops covered by the agreement. Many of the specific practices which underlie the agreement may be unknown, except in hazy form, even to the negotiators. Courts and arbitration in the context of most commercial contracts are resorted to because there has been a breakdown in the working relationship of the parties; such resort is the unwanted exception. But the grievance machinery under a collective bargaining agreement is at the very heart of the system of industrial self-government. Arbitration is the means of solving the unforeseeable by molding a system of private law for all the problems which may arise and to provide for their solution in a way which will generally accord with the variant needs and desires of the parties. The processing of disputes through the grievance machinery is actually a vehicle by which meaning and content is given to the collective bargaining agreement.

[SCOPE OF ARBITRATION CLAUSE]

Apart from matters that the parties specifically exclude, all of the questions on which the parties disagree must therefore come within the scope of the grievance and arbitration provisions of the collective agreement. The grievance procedure is, in other words, a part of the continuous collective bargaining process. It, rather than a strike, is the terminal point of a disagreement.

"A proper conception of the arbitrator's function is basic. He is not a public tribunal imposed upon the parties by superior authority which the parties are obliged to accept. He has no general charter to administer justice for a community which transcends the parties. He is rather part of a system of self-government created by and confined to the parties. . . ." Shulman, *supra*, at 1016.

The labor arbitrator performs functions which are not normal to the courts; the considerations which help him fashion judgments may indeed be foreign to the competence of courts. The labor arbitrator's source of law is not confined to the express provisions of the contract, as the industrial common law—the practices of the industry and the shop—is equally a part of the collective bargaining agreement although not expressed in it. The labor arbitrator is usually chosen because of the parties' confidence in his knowledge of the common law of the shop and their trust in his personal judgment to bring to bear considerations which are not expressed in the contract as criteria for judgment. The parties expect that his judgment of a particular grievance will reflect not only what the contract says but, insofar as the collective bargaining agreement permits, such factors as the effect upon productivity of a particular result, its consequence to the morale of the shop, his judgment whether tensions will be heightened or diminished. For the parties' objective in using the arbitration process is primarily to further their common goal of uninterrupted production under the agreement to make the agreement serve their specialized needs. The ablest judge cannot be expected to bring the same experience and competence to bear upon the determination of a grievance, because he cannot be similarly informed.

[JUDICIAL INQUIRY]

The Congress, however, has by § 301 of the Labor Management Relations Act, assigned the courts the duty of determining whether the reluctant party has breached his promise to arbitrate. For arbitration is a matter of contract and a party cannot be required to submit to arbitration any dispute which he has not agreed so to submit. Yet, to be consistent with congressional policy in favor of settlement of disputes by the parties through the machinery of arbitration, the judicial inquiry under § 301 must be strictly confined to question whether the reluctant party did agree to arbitrate the grievance or agreed to give the arbitrator power to make the award he made. An order to arbitrate the particular grievance should not be denied unless it may be said with positive assurance that arbitration clause is not susceptible to an interpretation that covers the asserted dispute. Doubts should be resolved in favor of coverage.[7]

We do not agree with the lower courts that contracting-out grievances were necessarily excepted from the grievance procedure of this agreement. To be sure the agreement provides that "matters which are strictly a function of management shall not be subject to arbitration." But it goes on to say that if "differences" arise or if "any local trouble of any kind" arises, the grievance procedure shall be applicable.

Collective bargaining agreements regulate or restrict the exercise of management functions; they do not oust management from the performance of them. Management hires and fires, pays and promotes, supervises and plans. All these are part of its function, and absent a collective bargaining agreement, it may be exercised freely except as limited by public law and by the willingness of employees to work under the particular, unilaterally imposed conditions. A collective bargaining agreement may treat only with certain specific practices, leaving the rest to management but subject to the possibility of work stoppages. When, however, an absolute no-strike clause is included in the agreement, then in a very real sense everything that management does is subject to the agreement, for either management is prohibited or limited in the action it takes, or if not, it is protected from interference by strikes. This comprehensive reach of the collective bargaining agreement does not mean, however, that the language, "strictly a function of management" has no meaning.

"Strictly a function of management" might be thought to refer to any practice of management in which, under particular circumstances prescribed by the agreement, it is permitted to indulge. But if courts, in order to determine arbitrability, were allowed to determine what is permitted and what is not, the arbitration clause would be swallowed up by the exception. Every grievance in a sense involves a claim that management has violated some provision of the agreement.

[FUNCTION OF MANAGEMENT]

Accordingly, "strictly a function of management" must be interpreted as referring only to that over which the contract gives management complete

---

[7]It is clear that under both the agreement in this case and that involved in *American Manufacturing Co.*, ante, 48 LRRM 2414, the question of arbitrability is for the courts to decide. Cf. Cox, Reflections Upon Labor Arbitration, 72 Harv. L. Rev. 1482, 1508–1509. Where the assertion by the claimant is that the parties excluded from court determination not merely the decision of the merits of the grievance but also the question of its arbitrability, vesting power to make both decisions in the arbitrator, the claimant must bear the burden of a clear demonstration of that purpose.

control and unfettered discretion. Respondent claims that the contracting-out of work falls within this category. Contracting-out work is the basis of many grievances: and that type of claim is grist in the mills of the arbitrators.[8] A specific collective bargaining agreement may exclude contracting-out from the grievance procedure. Or a written collateral agreement may make clear that contracting-out was not a matter for arbitration. In such a case a grievance based solely on contracting-out would not be arbitrable. Here, however, there is no such provision. Nor is there any showing that the parties designed the phrase "strictly a function of management" to encompass any and all forms of contracting-out. In the absence of any express provision excluding a particular grievance from arbitration, we think only the most forceful evidence of a purpose to exclude the claim from arbitration can prevail, particularly where, as here, the exclusion clause is vague and the arbitration clause quite broad. Since any attempt by a court to infer such a purpose necessarily comprehends the merits, the court should view with suspicion an attempt to persuade it to become entangled in the construction of the substantive provisions of a labor agreement, even through the back door of interpreting the arbitration clause, when the alternative is to utilize the services of an arbitrator.

The grievance alleged that the contracting-out was a violation of the collective bargaining agreement. There was, therefore, a dispute "as to the meaning and application of the provisions of this Agreement" which the parties had agreed would be determined by arbitration.

The judiciary sits in these cases to bring into operation an arbitral process which substitutes a regime of peaceful settlement for the older regime of industrial conflict. Whether contracting-out in the present case violated the agreement is the question. It is a question for the arbiter, not for the courts.

Reversed.

MR. JUSTICE FRANKFURTER concurs in the result.

MR. JUSTICE BLACK took no part in the consideration or decision of this case.

Dissenting Opinion

MR. JUSTICE WHITTAKER, dissenting.

---

[8]See *Celanese Corp. of America*, 33 LA 925, 941 (1959), where the arbiter in a grievance growing out of contracting-out work said:

"In my research I have located 64 published decisions which have been concerned with this issue covering a wide range of factual situations but all of them with the common characteristics— i.e., the contracting-out of work involved occurred under an Agreement that contained no provision that specifically mentioned contracting-out of work."

Until today, I have understood it to be the unquestioned law, as this Court has consistently held, that arbitrators are private judges chosen by the parties to decide particular matters specifically submitted;[1] that the contract under which matters are submitted to arbitrators is at once the source and limit of their authority and power;[2] and that their power to decide issues with finality, thus ousting the normal functions of the courts, must rest upon a clear, definitive agreement of the parties, as such powers can never be implied, *United States v. Moorman*, 338 U.S. 457, 462;[3] *Mercantile Trust Co. v. Hensey*, 205 U.S. 298, 309.[4] See also *Fernandez & Hnos v. Rickert Rice Mills*, 119 F. 2d 809, 815 (C.A. 1st Cir.);[5] *Marchant v. Mead-Morrison Mfg. Co.*, 252 N.Y. 284, 299, 169 N.E. 386, 391;[6] *Continental Milling & Feed Co. v. Doughnut Corp.*, 186 Md. 669, 48 A. 2d 447, 450;[7] *Jacob v. Weisser*, 207 Pa. 484, 56 A. 1065, 1067.[8] I believe that the Court today departs the established principles announced in these decisions.

Here, the employer operates a shop for the normal maintenance of its barges, but it is not equipped to make major repairs, and accordingly the employer has, from the beginning of its operations more than 19 years ago,

---

[1]"Arbitrators are judges chosen by the parties to decide the matter submitted to them." *Burchell v. Marsh*, 17 How. 334, 349.

[2]"The agreement under which [the arbitrators] were selected *was at once the source and limit of their authority*, and the award, to be binding, must in substance and form conform to the submission." *Continental Ins. Co. v. Garrett*, 125 F. 589, 590 (C.A. 6th Cir.)—Opinion by Judge, later Mr. Justice, Lurton. (Emphasis added.)

[3]"It is true that *the intention of the parties to submit their contractual disputes to final determination outside the courts should be made manifest by plain language.*" *United States v. Moorman*, 338 U.S. 457, 462. (Emphasis added.)

[4]"To make such [an arbitrator's] certificate conclusive *requires plain language in the contract. It is not to be implied.*" *Mercantile Trust Co. v. Hensey*, 205 U.S. 298, 309. (Emphasis added.)

[5]"A party is never required to submit to arbitration any question which he has not agreed so to submit, and contracts providing for arbritration *will be carefully construed in order not to force a party to submit to arbitration a question which he did not intend to be submitted.*" *Fernadez & Hnos v. Rickert Rice Mills*, 119 F. 2d 809, 815 (C.A. 1st Cir.). (Emphasis added.)

[6]In this leading case, Judge, later Mr. Justice, Cardozo said:
"This question is one of intention, to be ascertained by the same tests that are applied to contracts generally. . . . No one is under a duty to resort to these conventional tribunals, however helpful their processes, *except to the extent that he has signified his willingness.* Our own favor or disfavor of the cause of arbitration is not to count as a factor in the appraisal of the thought of others." *Marchant v. Mead-Morrison Mfg. Co.*, 252 N.Y. 284, 299, 169 N.E. 386, 391. (Emphasis added.)

[7]In this case, the Court, after quoting Judge Cardozo's language in *Marchant, supra*, saying that "the question is one of intention," said:
"Sound policy demands that the terms of an arbitration *must not be strained to discover power to pass upon matters in dispute, but the terms must be clear and unmistakable to oust the jurisdiction of the Court, for trial by jury cannot be taken away in any case merely by implication.*" *Continental Milling & Feed Co. v. Doughnut Corp.*, 186 Md. 669, 676, 48 A.2d 447, 450. (Emphasis added.)

[8]"But, under any circumstances, before the decision of an arbitrator can be held final and conclusive, it must appear, as was said in *Chandley Bros. v. Cambridge Springs*, 200 Pa. 230, 49 Atl. 772, *that power to pass upon the subject-matter is clearly given to him. 'The terms of the agreement are not to be strained to discover it. They must be clear and unmistakable to oust the jurisdiction of the courts; for trial by jury cannot be taken away by implication merely in any case.'*" *Jacob v. Weisser*, 207 Pa. 484, 489, 5 A. 1065, 107. (Emphasis added.)

contracted out its major work. During most, if not all, of this time the union has represented the employees in that unit. The District Court found that "[t]hroughout the successive labor agreements between these parties, including the present one, . . . [the union] has unsuccessfully sought to negotiate changes in the labor contract, and particularly during the negotiation of the present labor agreement, . . . which would have limited the right of the [employer] to continue the practice of contracting out such work." 168 F. Supp. 702, 704–705, 43 LRRM 2328.

[ARBITRATION CLAUSE]

The labor agreement involved here provides for arbitration of disputes respecting the interpretation and application of the agreement and, arguably, also some other things. But the first paragraph of the arbitration section says: "[M]atters which are strictly a function of management shall not be subject to arbitration under this section." Although acquiescing for 19 years in the employer's interpretation that contracting out work was "strictly a function of management," and having repeatedly tried—particularly in the negotiation of the agreement involved here—but unsuccessfully, to induce the employer to agree to a covenant that would prohibit it from contracting out work, the union, after having agreed to and signed the contract involved, presented a "grievance" on the ground that the employer's contracting out work, at a time when some employees in the unit were laid off for lack of work, constituted a partial "lockout" of employees in violation of the anti-lockout provision of the agreement.

Being unable to persuade the employer to agree to cease contracting out work or to agree to arbitrate the "grievance," the union brought this action in the District Court, under § 301 of the Labor Management Relations Act, 29 U.S.C. § 815, for a decree compelling the employer to submit the "grievance" to arbitration. The District Court, holding that the contracting out of work was, and over a long course of dealings had been interpreted and understood by the parties to be "strictly a function of management," and was therefore specifically excluded from arbitration by the terms of the contract, denied the relief prayed, 168 F. Supp. 702, 43 LRRM 2328. The Court of Appeals affirmed, 269 F. 2d 633, 44 LRRM 2567, and we granted certiorari. 361 U.S. 912.

The Court now reverses the judgment of the Court of Appeals. It holds that the arbitrator's source of law is "not confined to the express provisions of the contract," that arbitration should be ordered "unless it may be said with positive assurance that the arbitration clause is not susceptible to an interpretation that covers the asserted dispute," that "[d]oubts [of arbitrability] should be resolved in favor of coverage," and that when, as here, "a no-strike clause is included in the agreement, then . . . everything that management does is subject to [arbitration]." I understand the Court thus to hold that the arbitrators are not confined to the express provisions of the contract, that arbitration is to be ordered unless it may be said with positive assurance that arbitration of a particular dispute is excluded by the contract, that doubts of arbitrability are to be resolved in favor of arbitration, and that when, as here, the contract contains a no-strike clause, everything that management does is subject to arbitration.

[STRANGE DOCTRINE]

This is an entirely new and strange doctrine to me. I suggest, with deference, that it departs both the contract of the parties and the controlling decisions of this Court. I find nothing in the contract that purports to confer upon arbitrators any such general breadth of private judicial power. The Court cites no legislative or judicial authority that creates for or gives to arbitrators such broad general powers. And I respectfully submit that today's decision cannot be squared with the statement of Judge, later Mr. Justice, Cardozo in *Marchant* that "no one is under a duty to resort to these conventional tribunals, however helpful their process, *except to the extent that he has signified his willingness.* Our own favor or disfavor of the cause of arbitration is not to count as a factor in the appraisal of the thoughts of others," 252 N.Y., at 299, 169 N.E., at 391 (emphasis added); nor with his statement in that case that "[t]he question is one of intention, to be ascertained by the same tests that are applied to contracts generally," *id.,* nor with this Court's statement in *Moorman,* "that the intention of the parties to submit their contractual disputes to final determination outside the courts *should be made manifest by plain language,*" 338 U.S., at 462 (emphasis added); nor with this Court's statement in Hensey that: "To make such [an arbitrator's] certificate conclusive *requires plain language in the contract.* It is not to be implied." 205 U.S. at 309. (Emphasis added.) "A party is never required to submit to arbitration any question which he has not agreed so to submit, and *contracts providing for arbitration will be carefully construed in order not to force a party to submit to arbitration a question which he did not intend to be submitted.*" *Fernandez & Hnos v. Rickert Rice Mills, supra,* 119 F. 2d at 815 (C.A. 1st Cir). (Emphasis added.)

With respect, I submit that there is nothing in the contract here to indicate that the employer "signified [its] willingness" (*Marchant, supra,* at 391) to submit to arbitrators whether it must cease contracting out work. Certainly no such intention is "made manifest by plain language" (*Moorman, supra,* at 462), as the law "requires," because such consent "is not to be implied." (*Hensey, supra,* at 309). To the contrary, the parties by their conduct over many years interpreted the contracting out of major repair work to be "strictly a function of management," and if, as the concurring opinion suggests, the words of the contract can "be understood only by reference to the background which gave rise to their inclusion," then the interpretation given by the parties over 19 years to the phrase "matters which are strictly a function of management" should logically have some significance here. By their contract, the parties agreed that "matters which are strictly a function of management shall not be subject to arbitration." The union over the course of many years repeatedly tried to induce the employer to agree to a covenant prohibiting the contracting out of work, but was never successful. The union again made such an effort in negotiating the very contract involved here, and, failing of success, signed the contract, knowing, of course, that it did not contain any such covenant, but that, to the contrary, it contained, just as had the former contracts, a covenant that "matters which are strictly a function of management shall not be subject to arbitration." Does not this show that, instead of signifying a willingness to submit to arbitration the matter of whether the employer might continue to contract out work, the parties fairly agreed to exclude at least that matter from arbitration? Surely it cannot be said that the parties agreed to such a submission by any "plain language." *Moorman, supra,* at 462, and *Hensey, supra,* at 309. Does not then the Court's opinion compel the employer "to submit to arbitration [a] question which [it] has not agreed so to submit"? (*Fernandez & Hnos, supra,* at 815.)

[JUDICIAL QUESTION]

Surely the question whether a particular subject or class of subjects are or are not made arbitrable by a contract is a judicial question, and if, as the concurring opinion suggests, "the Court may conclude that [the contract] commits to arbitration any [subject or class of subjects]," it may likewise conclude that the contract does not commit such subject or class of subjects to arbitration, and "[w]ith that finding the Court will have exhausted its function" no more nor less by denying arbitration than by ordering it. Here the District Court found, and the Court of Appeals approved its finding, that by the terms of the contract, as interpreted by the parties over 19 years, the contracting out of work was "strictly a function of management" and "not subject to arbitration." That finding, I think, should be accepted here. Acceptance of it requires affirmance of the judgment.

I agree with the Court that courts have no proper concern with the "merits" of claims which by contract the parties have agreed to submit to the exclusive jurisdiction of arbitrators. But the question is one of jurisdiction. Neither may entrench upon the jurisdiction of the other. The test is: Did the parties in their contract "manifest by plain language" (*Moorman, supra,* at 462) their willingness to submit the issue in controversy to arbitrators? If they did, then the arbitrators have exclusive jurisdiction of it, and the courts, absent fraud or the like, must respect that exclusive jurisdiction and cannot interfere. But if they did not, then the courts must exercise their jurisdiction, when properly invoked, to protect the citizen against the attempted use by arbitrators of pretended powers actually never conferred. That question always is, and from its very nature msut be, a judicial one. Such was the question presented to the District Court and the Court of Appeals here. They found the jurisdictional facts, properly applied the settled law to those facts, and correctly decided the case. I would therefore affirm the judgment.

United Steelworkers of America v. Enterprise Wheel and Car Corporation

Supreme Court of the United States
363 U.S. 593, 46 LRRM 2423 (1960)

Full Text of Opinion

MR. JUSTICE DOUGLAS delivered the opinion of the Court.

Petitioner union and respondent during the period relevant here had a collective bargaining agreement which provided that any differences "as to the meaning and application" of the agreement should be submitted to arbitration and that the arbitrator's decision "shall be final and binding on the parties." Special provisions were included concerning the suspension and discharge of employees. The agreement stated:

"Should it be determined by the Company or by an arbitrator in accordance with the grievance procedure that the employee has been suspended unjustly or discharged in violation of the provisions of this Agreement, the Company shall reinstate the employee and pay full compensation at the employee's regular rate of pay for the time lost."

The agreement also provided:

". . . It is understood and agreed that neither party will institute *civil suits or legal proceedings* against the other for alleged violation of any of the provisions of this labor contract; instead all disputes will be settled in the manner outlined in this Article III—Adjustment of Grievances."

[FACTS OF CASE]

A group of employees left their jobs in protest against the discharge of one employee. A union official advised them at once to return to work. An official of respondent at their request gave them permission and then rescinded it. The next day they were told they did not have a job any more "until this thing was settled one way or the other."

A grievance was filed; and when respondent finally refused to arbitrate, this suit was brought for specific enforcement of the arbitration provisions of the agreement. The District court ordered arbitration. The arbitrator found that the discharge of the men was not justified, though their conduct, he said, was improper. In his view the facts warranted at most a suspension of the men for 10 days each. After their discharge and before the arbitration award the collective bargaining agreement had expired. The union, however, continued to represent the workers at the plant. The arbitrator rejected the contention that expiration of the agreement barred reinstatement of the employees. He held that the provision of the agreement above quoted imposed an unconditional obligation on the employer. He awarded reinstatement with back pay, minus pay for a 10-day suspension and such sums as these employees received from other employment.

Respondent refused to comply with the award. Petitioner moved the District Court for enforcement. The District Court directed respondent to comply. 168 F. Supp. 308, 43 LRRM 2291. The Court of Appeals, while agreeing that the District Court had jurisdiction to enforce an arbitration award under a collective bargaining agreement,[1] held that the failure of the award to specify the amounts to be deducted from the back pay rendered the award unenforceable. That defect, it agreed could be remedied by requiring the parties to complete the arbitration. It went on to hold, however, that an award for back pay subsequent to the date of termination of the collective bargaining agreement could not be enforced. It also held that the requirement for reinstatement of the discharged employees was likewise unenforceable because the collective agreement had expired. 269 F. 2d 327, 44 LRRM 2349.

[MERITS OF AWARDS]

The refusal of courts to review the merits of an arbitration award is the proper approach to arbitration under collective bargaining agreements. The federal policy of settling labor disputes by arbitration would be undermined if courts had the final say on the merits of the awards. As we stated in *United Steelworkers of America v. Warrior & Gulf Navigation Co.*, *ante*, 46 LRRM 2416, decided this day, the arbitrators under these collective agreements are indispensable agencies in a continuous collective bargaining process. They sit to settle disputes at the plant level—disputes that require for their solution knowledge of the custom and practices of a particular factory or of a particular industry as reflected in particular agreements.[2]

---

[1]See *Textile Workers v. Cone Mills Corp.*, 268 F. 2d 920, 44 LRRM 2345 (C.A. 4th Cir.).

[2]"Persons unfamiliar with mills and factories—farmers or professors, for example—often remark upon visiting them that they seem like another world. This is particularly true if, as in the steel industry, both tradition and technology have strongly and uniquely molded the ways men think and act when at work. The newly hired employee, the 'green hand,' is gradually initiated into what amounts to a miniature society. There he finds himself in a strange environment that assaults his senses with unusual sounds and smells and often with different 'weather conditions' such as sudden drafts of heat, cold, or humidity. He discovers that the society of which he only gradually becomes a part has of course a formal government of its own—the rules which management and the union have laid down—but that it also differs from or parallels the world outside in social classes, folklore, ritual, and traditions.

"Under the process in the old mills a very real 'miniature society' has grown up, and in important ways the technological revolution described in this case history shattered it. But a new society or work community was born immediately, though for a long time it developed slowly. As the old society was strongly molded by the *discontinuous* process of making pipe, so was the new one molded by the *continuous* process and strongly influenced by the characteristics of new highspeed automatic equipment." Walker, Life in the Automatic Factory, 3 Harv. Bus. Rev. 111, 117.

When an arbitrator is commissioned to interpret and apply the collective bargaining agreement, he is to bring his informed judgment to bear in order to reach a fair solution of a problem. This is especially true when it comes to formulating remedies. There the need is for flexibility in meeting a wide variety of situations. The draftsmen may never have thought of what specific remedy should be awarded to meet a particular contingency. Nevertheless, an arbitrator is confined to interpretation and application of the collective bargaining agreement; he does not sit to dispense his own brand of industrial justice. He may of course look for guidance from many sources, yet his award is legitimate only so long as it draws its essence from the collective bargaining agreement. When the arbitrator's words manifest an infidelity to this obligation, courts have no choice but to refuse enforcement of the award.

[OPINION OF ARBITRATOR]

The opinion of the arbitrator in this case, as it bears upon the award of back pay beyond the date of the agreement's expiration and reinstatement, is ambiguous. It may be read as based solely upon the arbitrator's view of the requirements of enacted legislation, which would mean that he exceeded the scope of the submission. Or it may be read as embodying a construction of the agreement itself, perhaps with the arbitrator looking to "the law" for help in determining the sense of the agreement. A mere ambiguity in the opinion accompanying an award, which permits the inference that the arbitrator may have exceeded his authority, is not a reason for refusing to enforce the award. Arbitrators have no obligation to the court to give their reasons for an award. To require opinions[3] free of ambiguity may lead arbitrators to play it safe by writing no supporting opinions. This would be undesirable for a well reasoned opinion tends to engender confidence in the integrity of the process and aids in clarifying the underlying agreement. Moreover, we see no reason to assume that this arbitrator has abused the trust the parties confided in him and has not stayed within the areas marked out for his consideration. It is not apparent that he went beyond the submission. The Court of Appeal's opinion refusing to enforce the reinstatement and partial back pay portions of the award was not based upon any finding that the arbitrator did not premise his award on his construction of the contract. It merely disagreed with the arbitrator's construction of it.

The collective bargaining agreement could have provided that if any of the employees were wrongfully discharged, the remedy would be reinstatement and back pay up to the date they were returned to work. Respondent's major argument seems to be that by applying correct principles of law to the interpretation of the collective bargaining agreement it can be determined

---

[3]See Jalet, "Judicial Review of Arbitration: The Judicial Attitude," 45 Cornell L. Q. 519, 522.

that the agreement did not so provide, and that therefore the arbitrator's decision was not based upon the contract. The acceptance of this view would require courts, even under the standard arbitration clause, to review the merits of every construction of the contract. This plenary review by a court of the merits would make meaningless the provisions that the arbitrator's decision is final, for in reality it would almost never be final. This underlines the fundamental error which we have alluded to in *United States Steelworkers of America v. American Manufacturing Co.*, *ante*, 46 LRRM 2414, decided this day. As we there emphasized the question of interpretation of the collective bargaining agreement is a question for the arbitrator. It is the arbitrator's construction which was bargained for; and so far as the arbitrator's decision concerns construction of the contract, the courts have no business overruling him because their interpretation of the contract is different from his.

We agree with the Court of Appeals that the judgment of the District Court should be modified so that the amounts due the employees may be definitely determined by arbitration. In all other respects we think the judgment of the District Court should be affirmed. Accordingly, we reverse the judgment of the Court of Appeals, except for that modification, and remand the case to the District Court for proceedings in conformity with this opinion.

It is so ordered.

Mr. Justice Frankfurter concurs in the result.

Mr. Justice Black took no part in the consideration or decision of this case.

Dissenting Opinion

Mr. Justice Whittaker, dissenting.

Claiming that the employer's discharge on January 18, 1957, of 11 employees violated the provisions of its collective bargaining contract with the employer—covering the period beginning April 5, 1956, and ending April 5, 1957—the union sought and obtained arbitration, under the provisions of the contract, of the issues whether these employees had been discharged in violation of the agreement and, if so, should be ordered reinstated and awarded wages from the time of their wrongful discharge. In August 1957, more than four months after the collective agreement had expired, these issues were tried before and submitted to a Board of Arbitrators. On April 10, 1958, the arbitrators made their award, finding that the 11 employees had been discharged in violation of the agreement and ordering their reinstatement with back pay at their regular rates from a time 10 days after their discharge to the time of reinstatement. Over the employer's objection that the collective agreement and the submission under it did not authorize nor empower the arbitrators to award reinstatement or wages for any period after the date of expiration of the contract (April 5, 1957), the District Court ordered enforcement of the award. The Court of Appeals modified the judgment by eliminating the requirement that the employer reinstate the employees and pay them wages for the period *after* expiration of the collective agreement, and affirmed it in all other respects, 269 F. 2d 327, 44 LRRM 2349, and we granted certiorari, 361 U.S. 929.

That the propriety of the discharges, under the collective agreement, was arbitrable under the provisions of that agreement, even after its expiration, is not in issue. Nor is there any issue here as to the power of the arbitrators to award reinstatement status and back pay to the discharged employees to the date of expiration of the collective agreement. It is conceded, too, that the collective agreement expired by its terms on April 5, 1957, and was never extended or renewed.

The sole question here is whether the arbitrators exceeded the submission and their powers in awarding reinstatement and back pay for any period after expiration of the collective agreements. Like the Court of Appeals, I think they did. I find nothing in the collective agreement that purports to so authorize. Nor does the Court point to anything in the agreement that purports to do so. Indeed, the union does not contend that there is any such covenant in the contract. Doubtless all rights that accrued to the employees under the collective agreement during its term, and that were made arbitrable by its provisions, could be awarded to them by the arbitrators, even though the period of the agreement had ended. But surely no rights *accrued* to the employees under the agreement after it had expired. Save for the provisions of the collective agreement, and in the absence, as here, of any applicable rule of law or contrary covenant between the employer and the employees, the employer had the legal right to discharge the employees at will. The collective agreement, however, protected them against discharge, for specified reasons, during its continuation. But when that agreement expired, it did not continue to afford rights *in futuro* to the employees—as though still effective and governing. After the agreement expired the government status of these 11 employees was terminable at the will of the employer, as the Court of Appeals quite properly held, 269 F. 2d, at 331, 44 LRRM 2349, and see *Meadows v. Radio Industries*, 222 F. 2d 347, 349, 36 LRRM 2147 (C.A. 7th Cir.); *Atchison, T. & S. F. R. Co. v. Andrews*, 211 F. 2d 264, 265 (C.A. 10th Cir.); *Warden v. Hinds*, 163 F. 201 (C.A. 4th Cir.), and the announced discharge of these 11 employees then became lawfully effective.

Once the contract expired, no rights continued to accrue under it to the employees. Thereafter they had no contractual right to demand that the employer continue to employ them, and *a fortiori* the arbitrators did not have power to order the employer to do so; nor did the arbitrators have power to order the employer to pay wages to them after the date of termination of the contract, which was also the effective date of their discharges.

The judgment of the Court of Appeals, affirming so much of the award as required reinstatement of the 11 employees to employment status and payment of their wages until expiration of the contract, but not thereafter, seems to me to be indubitably correct, and I would affirm it.

Concurring Opinion

[To decisions in *United Steelworkers v. American Mfg. Co.; United Steelworkers v. Warrior and Gulf Navigation Co.;* and *United Steelworkers v. Enterprise Wheel and Car Corp.*]

MR. JUSTICE BRENNAN, with whom MR. JUSTICE HARLAN joins, concurring.

While I join the Court's opinions in Nos. 443, 360 and 538, I add a word in Nos. 443 and 360.

In each of these two cases the issue concerns the enforcement of but one promise—the promise to arbitrate in the context of an agreement dealing with a particular subject matter, the industrial relations between employers and employees. Other promises contained in the collective bargaining agreements are beside the point unless, by the very terms of the arbitration promise, they are made relevant to its interpretation. And I emphasize this, for the arbitration promise is itself a contract. The parties are free to make that promise as broad or as narrow as they wish for there is no compulsion in law requiring them to include any such promise in their agreement. The meaning of the arbitration promise is not to be found simply by reference to the dictionary definitions of the words the parties use, or by reference to the interpretation of commercial arbitration clauses. Words in a collective bargaining agreement, rightly viewed by the Court to be the charter instrument of a system of industrial self-government, like words in a statute, are to be understood only by reference to the background which gave rise to their inclusion. The Court therefore avoids the prescription of inflexible rules for the enforcement of arbitration promises. Guidance is given by identifying the various considerations which a court should take into account when construing a particular clause—considerations of the milieu in which the clause is negotiated and of the national labor policy. It is particularly underscored that the arbitral process in collective bargaining presupposes that the parties wanted the informed judgment of an arbitrator, precisely for the reason that judges cannot provide it. Therefore, a court asked to enforce a promise to arbitrate should ordinarily refrain from involving itself in the interpretation of the substantive provisions of the contract.

[QUESTION FOR COURT]

To be sure, since arbitration is a creature of contract, a court must always inquire, when a party seeks to invoke its aid to force a reluctant party to the arbitration table, whether the parties have agreed to arbitrate the particular dispute. In this sense, the question of whether a dispute is "abitrable" is inescapably for the court.

On examining the arbitration clause, the court may conclude that it commits to arbitration any "dispute, difference, disagreement, or controversy of any nature or character." With that finding the court will have exhausted its function, except to order the reluctant party to arbitration. Similarly, although the arbitrator may be empowered only to interpret and apply the contract, the parties may have provided that any dispute as to whether a particular claim is within the arbitration clause is itself for the arbitrator. Again the court, without more, must send any dispute to the arbitrator, for the parties have agreed that the construction of the arbitration promise itself is for the arbitrator, and the reluctant party has breached his promise by refusing to submit the dispute to arbitration.

[AMERICAN CASE]

In *American*, the Court deals with a request to enforce the "standard" form of arbitration clause, one that provides for the arbitration of "any disputes, misunderstandings, differences or grievances arising between the parties as to the meaning, interpretation and application of this agreement. . . ." Since the arbitration clause itself is part of the agreement, it might be argued that a dispute as to the meaning of that clause is for the arbitrator. But the Court rejects this position, saying that the threshold question, the meaning of the arbitration clause itself, is for the judge unless the parties clearly state to the contrary. However, the Court finds that the meaning of that "standard" clause is simply that the parties have agreed to arbitrate any dispute which the moving party asserts to involve construction of the substantive provisions of the contract, because such a dispute necessarily does involve such a construction.

[WARRIOR CASE]

The issue in the *Warrior* case is essentially no different from that in *American*, that is, it is whether the company agreed to arbitrate a particular grievance. In contrast to *American*, however, the arbitration promise here excludes a particular area from arbitration—"matters which are strictly a function of management." Because the arbitration promise is different, the scope of the court's inquiry may be broader. Here, a court may be required to examine the substantive provisions of the contract to ascertain whether the parties have provided that contracting out shall be a "function of management." If a court may delve into the merits to the extent of inquiring whether the parties have expressly agreed whether or not contracting-out was a "function of management," why was it error for the lower court here to evaluate the evidence of bargaining history for the same purpose? Neat logical distinctions do not provide the answer. The Court rightly concludes that appropriate regard for the national labor policy and the special factors relevant to the labor arbitral process, admonish that judicial inquiry into the merits of this grievance should be limited to the search for an explicit provision which brings the grievance under the cover of the exclusion clause since "the exclusion clause is vague and arbitration clause quite broad." The hazard of going further into the merits is amply demonstrated by what the courts below did. On the basis of inconclusive evidence, those courts found that *Warrior* was in no way limited by any implied covenants of good faith and fair dealing from contracting out as it pleased—which would necessarily mean that *Warrior* was free completely to destroy the collective bargaining agreement by contracting out all the work.

The very ambiguity of the *Warrior* exclusion clause suggests that the parties were generally more concerned with having an arbitrator render decisions as to the meaning of the contract than they were in restricting the arbitrator's jurisdiction. The case might of course be otherwise were the arbitration clause very narrow, or the exclusion clause quite specific, for the inference might then be permissible that the parties had manifested a greater interest in confining the arbitrator; the presumption of arbitrability would then not have the same force and the Court would be somewhat freer to examine into the merits.

The Court makes reference to an arbitration clause being the *quid pro quo* for a no-strike clause. I do not understand the Court to mean that the application of the principles announced today depends upon the presence of a no-strike clause in the agreement.

MR. JUSTICE FRANKFURTER joins these observations.

Appendix C
Sample of Subpoena

The following illustrative subpoena was prepared to comply with California state law:

IN ARBITRATION PROCEEDINGS PURSUANT TO
THE COLLECTIVE BARGAINING AGREEMENT BETWEEN
THE PARTIES

```
                              )
                              )
                              )
                              )
                              )
                              )          SUBPOENA
                              )
                              )
                              )
                              )
                              )
_____ )
```

GREETINGS TO:

PLEASE TAKE NOTICE that you are hereby ordered to appear before KATHY KELLY, Arbitrator, at the arbitration hearing in the above entitled matter on _____ at 9:00 a.m., at 544 Market Street, Suite 401, San Francisco, California, to testify as a witness in this action. You must appear at that time and place unless you make a special agreement to appear at another time or place with _____, representative of the _____ who can be reached at _____.

[For a Subpoena Duces Tecum, requiring the production of documents, add the following language: "And you are hereby required to bring with you and produce at said time and place (unless other arrangements are made), the books, records, correspondence and documents more fully and specifically described in the attached declaration of _____." (The declaration should establish the relevance of the documents, the existence of good cause for their production and the fact that they are in the possession of the person subpoenaed).]

CONTACT the representative requesting this subpoena, listed above, on or before the date on which you are required to appear, if you have any question about the time or date for you to appear, or if you want to be certain that your presence is required.

Pursuant to California Code of Civil Procedure, Section 2065, you are hereby notified that you may claim witness fees in the amount of $35.00 plus mileage actually traveled, both ways, at the rate of $.20 per mile. The compensation required by the Government Code has been deposited with the Arbitrator [required only if the witness is a government employee such as a police officer]. You may make such claim to the person serving this Subpoena or to the above-named counsel before or at the time of the hearing.*

Your disobedience to this Subpoena may be punished by a court. Your disobedience to this Subpoena also may result in your forfeiture to the _____ of the sum of Five Hundred Dollars ($500.00), as well as all damages which the _____ may sustain by reason of your failure to comply with this Subpoena.

Dated: _____   _____

Kathy Kelly

---

*Check state law since it may be different from California law.

Appendix D
Submission Agreements

In Grievance Arbitration:

Where the agreement contains an arbitration clause, the arbitration itself is triggered by the notice provided for in the arbitration clause. That clause may contain the details as to procedure and the arbitrator's authority. Generally, all such arbitration clauses provide that the arbitrator may not change or add to the terms of the agreement, and that the arbitrator's decision shall be final and binding. Some of the arbitration clauses are specific as to the right to availability of witnesses; the right to cross-examine witnesses; whether the grievance is submitted to a single arbitrator or a board of arbitration; that the arbitrator or board of arbitration shall submit an opinion with the decision.

In cases where the arbitration clause does not specify procedure, practice is followed and coincides with those procedures noted above.

Generally, a formal submission agreement for the arbitration of grievances is not used. It is sufficient to launch the arbitration of a grievance by simply sending the proper notice requesting arbitration as provided in the arbitration agreement.

Some parties do agree to formal submission agreements for the arbitration of a grievance. Such an agreement follows:

IN ARBITRATION PROCEEDINGS
BEFORE JOHN KAGEL, ESQ.

In the Matter of Controversy)	
between)	
B COMPANY,)	Arbitration Case
and)	No. 130
LOCAL UNION NO. 1245,)	SUBMISSION AGREEMENT
Re: Prearranged Overtime)	

In accordance with Title 102, Step Six of the Labor Agreement between B COMPANY and LOCAL UNION NO. 1245, (hereinafter "the parties"), the parties enter into the following Submission Agreement regarding that grievance designated as Review Committee File Nos. 1603-84-38 and 1610-85-3 (hereinafter "grievance"), which the parties hereby agree to submit to arbitration pursuant to Title 102 of the Labor Agreement.

1. The grievance, and the arbitration proceedings held pursuant to this Submission Agreement, shall be referred to as Arbitration Case No. 130.

2. The parties have selected John Kagel, Esq., to serve as Chairperson for the arbitration proceedings. Two (2) Company and two (2) Union members will advise and consult with the Chairperson and will sit with him as a Board of Arbitration (hereinafter "Board") in hearing the grievance. The parties may at any time make substitutions in the representatives each originally named to serve on the Board. The parties may waive the attendance of either or both of their respective members at meetings of the Board and at the hearing to be held before the Board.

3. The grievance has been pursued through the grievance procedure contained in the Labor Agreement and is properly before the Board for hearing and decision.

4. The Board shall resolve only the ultimate issue involved in the grievance and those issues which must necessarily be decided in order to resolve the ultimate issue. The specific ultimate issue involved in the grievance is stated hereafter.

5. The Board shall hold a hearing, or hearings, at which the parties may present evidence and arguments in support of their respective positions regarding the issue before the Board for resolution. Formal notice need not be given of the time and place of the hearing. The hearing shall commence at 245 Market Street in the 14th floor conference room at 10:00 a.m. on April 24, 1985 and shall, if the Board deems necessary, continue at times and locations as the Board shall decide. Upon showing of good cause, any hearing date shall be changed at the request of either party, or the Chairperson.

6. There will be submitted to the Board in connection with the grievance copies of the Labor Agreement and this Submission Agreement which shall be marked and introduced into evidence as Joint Exhibits 1 and 2, respectively.

7. The hearings shall be informal, but will allow for the orderly presentation of each party's case.

Notwithstanding any provisions of the Labor Agreement that may be construed to the contrary, employees attending the hearing at the Union's demand or request shall be excused from work without pay.

8. The parties may at any time agree among themselves to resolve the issue involved in this arbitration case and to withdraw it from arbitration and from the Board.

9. The Chairperson shall have the right and obligation to render a separate written decision in this arbitration case, together with a written opinion setting forth the reasoning and analysis by which he arrived at the decision. When two (2) of the other members of the Board concur in the decision, that decision shall be final and binding upon the parties unless the decision adds to or modifies any of the provisions of the Labor Agreement, or the arbitration proceedings and/or the decision is contrary to applicable law governing arbitration.

A signed copy of the decision shall be served on both parties by the Chairperson, either personally or by registered or certified mail.

10. The Company and Union will share equally the expense of providing a stenographic transcript of the hearing and in fees and expenses of the Chairperson in connection with this arbitration. All other costs and expenses will be borne by the party incurring them.

ISSUE

Was the Company's unilateral termination of a local prearranged overtime practice a violation of the Agreement? If so, what is the remedy?

Dated: _____   Dated: _____
Signed: _____   Signed: _____
                                    LOCAL UNION NO. 1245

The suggestion that a written submission agreement be drafted may seem too formal in its approach. But observing this suggestion would require the parties to meet together and negotiate the terms of such an agreement. Such a negotiation could lead to a settlement without the need of going to arbitration. This can result when the parties seek to define and agree upon the specific issue to be arbitrated. They may find that they are not too far apart for a negotiated settlement. In short, it provides another opportunity to settle the dispute without going to arbitration. This prophylactic result that may flow from negotiating the submission agreement is of great importance.

Additionally, by formally negotiating the agreement, the parties can sharpen the issues they desire to arbitrate. And the authority of the arbitrator is thus more specifically defined. Finally, much time can be saved at the hearings if the preliminary work involved in drafting the contents of a submission agreement is done prior to the arbitration.

In Interest Arbitration:

A submission agreement in interest arbitration, that is, concerning the terms of the collective bargaining agreement, is always required. The existing collective bargaining agreement concerns itself with arbitration of grievances relating to already agreed-upon terms of the agreement.

Such a submission agreement should contain provisions that the parties agree to arbitrate specifically stated issues. For example, if one of the issues concerns wages, the company proposal and union proposal should be set forth in parallel columns, and it should be stated that the arbitrator's authority is limited to the specific proposal of each party or any variance between such proposals. And that the arbitrator's decision shall be final and binding.

To provide that an award is "final and binding" does not necessarily mean that the parties have waived such legal rights as they may have under appropriate law. A party may, under certain circumstances, go to court for the purposes of modifying or correcting an award, or to have an award vacated.

Additionally, such a submission agreement should provide for the procedural details of the arbitration, similar to those observed in grievance arbitration.

Appendix E
Re Transcripts*

One . . . [practice] which is prevalent in arbitration is the failure of arbitrators to give parties a fair and full hearing because they do not have a transcript of the hearing.

An arbitrator is duty bound to make his or her decision based on the record of the case, . . . [a] transcript of the hearing is the only official record of the hearing. Yet, the American Arbitration Association publication "Labor Arbitration—What You Need to Know," states that while transcripts are permitted under the AAA rules, "they should be ordered reluctantly." One reason for the "reluctance" is the statement that, "The arbitrator may then feel obliged to refer to it in preparing the opinion." This is an astounding statement, since it is the obligation of the arbitrator to write his [or her] opinion and then make a decision based on the official record of the case—the transcript.

What is the alternative? Note-taking and tapes taken by arbitrators? . . .

. . .

Yet the AAA, in its publication entitled, "Study Time" of January 1984, with reference to note-taking by arbitrators, stated:

Note-takers are faced with a seemingly impossible task. They must write down what has just been said, while listening to what is now being said. Consequently, many note-takers feel that they are always lagging behind.

The article further said:

To overcome this difficulty, experts advise them to reduce their writing to the skill of an automatic skill. In this way, it will be possible to do two things at one time.

---

*These comments concerning the use of transcripts in arbitration proceedings are from a paper delivered by Sam Kagel at the meeting of the National Academy of Arbitrators, May 31, 1985. See Kagel, "Legalism in Arbitration: I. Legalism—and Some Comments on Illegalism—in Arbitration," in W.J. Gershenfeld (ed.), *Arbitration 1985: Law and Practice, Proceedings of the 38th Annual Meeting of the National Academy of Arbitrators*, 180–191 (BNA Books, 1986).

The complete absurdity of suggesting that arbitrators should reduce their note writing to the level of an "automatic skill," so they can do two things at one time, is self-evident. This AAA publication quotes a number of arbitrators, all of whom indicate their trials and tribulations and difficulties and concerns about note-taking.

. . . [T]he arbitrator's opinion and decision is supposed to be based upon the entire record of the hearing. The record of the hearing is not the notes taken by the arbitrator. . . . something may be testified to during the third hour of the hearing, contrasted with what might have been said during the first hour which could be the turning point in a particular case, and the note-taker may not have that relevant entry made during the first hour of the hearing. There is no way of knowing that the note-taker would have such an entry or be able to recall it accurately without a note.

A grievant is entitled to know why he or she lost or won a case. The union and the employer are entitled to the same right. The arbitrator's opinion must reflect accurately and completely the basis for the decision. . . .

An arbitrator's notes could not serve such a purpose. The losing party would believe, correctly or not, that the arbitrator's notes did not contain material supporting its position.

. . .

. . . [C]onsider the role of transcripts when courts may be reviewing arbitrators' decisions. In this regard, . . . note a few pertinent court cases.

In *Swift Packing Company v. Food Workers Local 1* [115 LRRM 3256 (N.D. N.Y. 1983)], the Union sought to have the arbitration award vacated, and one of the grounds was "the arbitrator's refusal to hear certain testimony." The Court stated: "A fair reading of the *transcript* discloses beyond any question that the arbitrator did not in any sense 'refuse' to hear plaintiff's evidence." (Emphasis supplied)

In *Wood v. Teamsters Local 406* [583 F. Supp. 1471, 117 LRRM 2618 (W.D. Mich. 1984)], footnote 4 reads:

Some courts allowed arbitrators to be questioned regarding what occurred at the arbitration hearing. See *Blinik v. International Harvester Company*, 87 F.R.D. 490 (N.D. Ill. 1980). In the instant case, a *transcript* of the hearing exists and it therefore is not necessary to question the arbitrator for this purpose. (Emphasis supplied)

In *Chemical Workers Local 566 v. Mobay Chemical* [118 LRRM 2859 (4th Cir. 1985)], the issue was whether the arbitrator could consider matters beyond those contained in a letter of discharge. And, in this case, the court, quoting extensively from the *transcript* of the case, found consent by both parties to the issue and upheld the arbitrator's award.

In *Laborers v. U.S. Postal Service* [118 LRRM 2216 (6th Cir. 1985)], the court was concerned with alleged misconduct on the part of the arbitrator, and the court pointed out:

No verbatim record that might shed clear light on these allegations was kept of the . . . arbitration hearing.

In that case, the district court had held an evidentiary hearing; in effect, reheard the case, at least as it related to the alleged misconduct of the arbitrator. Whether other district courts would go so far is uncertain. It is clearly contrary to the purposes of arbitration to prolong the process and allow the arbitrator to be so "second-guessed."

. . . [I]n *Alexander v. Gardner-Denver*, the Supreme Court stated that it would not defer to arbitration decisions in cases where arbitrators have ruled against grievants claiming discrimination. But, it is significant that the Court in Footnote 21 stated that weight could be accorded arbitration decisions if certain relevant factors were present, among them an *"adequate record."* An arbitrator's notes, or even tapes, would not, in my opinion, be such an "adequate record" so as to satisfy a court. I am familiar with cases where transcripts of arbitrations, when introduced in such court proceedings, have led to the dismissal of actions under *Alexander.* And, at least in such instances, the courts have deferred to the arbitrator's decisions.

And let's take the case where arbitrators act as such in pension or health and welfare cases. They are considered in such cases to be fiduciaries by the Department of Labor. If an attack is made on such an arbitrator's decision, again, only a transcript would be of value in actually reflecting what occurred at the hearing, as well as the arbitrator's conduct, and the basis for the decision. It should be noted that in this kind of case, arbitrators expose themselves to possible monetary damages if they are considered fiduciaries.

A transcript then is essential to aid the arbitrator in making a decision based on the record, and to provide protection against attacks that may be made on his decisions.

What about the value of a transcript when the union and its counsel may be sued on the basis of having breached their duty of fair representation, and the employer is charged with having wrongfully discharged the grievants? Such a suit followed a decision I had made sustaining the discharge of three grievants.

In deciding that matter, in *Balestreri v. Western Carloading* [112 LRRM 2628 (N. D. Cal. 1980)], the court issued a summary judgment in favor of the defendants. The court made specific reference to the transcript of the hearing as its basis for making key findings in favor of the defendants. Notes of the hearing could not have served such a purpose.

In short, one of the key elements of a fair and full hearing requires, in my opinion, that a transcript of the hearing be made to:

1. protect the process;

2. protect the grievant;

3. protect the employer and the union;

4. protect the arbitrator; and

5. protect whoever is acting as counsel.

. . .

With reference to the expense of a transcript, let me emphasize that it is the arbitrator who controls the process. And, there are many *better* ways for an arbitrator to control the expense of the process than by not having a transcript. Arbitrators are responsible for the conduct of their hearing. Cumulative evidence should not be permitted. Irrelevant arguments or discussions should be kept off the record. Parties should be encouraged, if not directed, to agree on the issues and stipulations of facts and records prior to the beginning of the hearing. The arbitrator should control the hearing, not counsel.

Index

1105